EMOTIONAL BARRIERS BETWEEN YOU & YOUR CHILD

PRACTICAL PARENTING TIPS

ALAN JOSEPH

Copyright © Alan Joseph
All Rights Reserved.

This book is dedicated to my parents,

Mr. Savariraj and Mrs. Elisarani

Contents

Contents

Foreword

Psychology in the area of Parenting is a fast-emerging field. Professionals in medicine and psychology come together to focus on the earliest stages of human life-from preconception through lifespan. Thirty years of worldwide clinical research supports the ancient Indian knowing that the beginning of life is the most important and impressionable. Psychological problems and illness start this early. Therefore, understanding what children really need can form a protection against physical illness, mental illness, and suffering throughout their life.

People's earliest experiences imprint and become the subconscious programming. Childhood is the time of building the foundations of a health body, emotions, and relationships. These established patterns are at the root of many health, relationship, emotional/psychological and learning problems seen as all ages.

Over the years that I have practised psychotherapy, many of my clients only got real relief from their pain when we worked on these early issues. I came to realize how difficult this was and how few adults would or could ever go this deep into themselves. At this point I began to think in terms of prevention. If parents could better understand what children need, and give it to them at the appropriate time, so much pain and illness could be prevented.

It is this view of psychology which Mr. Alan is deeply committed to. The book " **Emotional Barriers between You & Your child**", not only benefits from the author's empirical studies, but it also gains from his academic and practical experience in teaching. His experience has contributed to her understanding of parenting. During recent years, he has also been exposed to a wide number of clients which provided him with a good basis to engage in intense studies.

This book is enthusiastic celebration of parenthood and child upbringing. I think that this book will have numerous readers who will have gained a broader perspective of pregnancy and child upbringing. It explores the psychology of children in terms of positive parenting, setting limits, positive discipline, problem behaviour, using mobile, tv and social media wisely, having dialogue, decision making, sibling rivalry, resolving conflicts, and evolving character, conscience, and values. There are signposts in these pages. Readers can use them to find their way to great treasures.

This book makes a remarkable contribution to the understanding of child upbringing. Academics, scholars, prospective or parents, counsellors and psychotherapists may all find this book stimulating.

Fr.Wilson
Anugraha Director
Capuchin Institute for Counselling and Psychotherapy
Dindidul , TamilNadu

Preface

Only if the child is in good physical health and in a harmonious mental state during the period of growth i.e childhood, he/she will live a happy life in the future. Depression is just like any other illness, but it gets deep rooted in young minds and leaves a long lasting mark of it through life. We, as adults, can understand this with personal experiences. In today's modern times, international companies, educational institutions and many other offices, for senior citizens, sick people, orphans, families and children, psychological counselling is a must and need of the hour.

This book has been compiled through the experience of a psychological counsellor and is easily understandable by everyone. This book is divided into 4 parts. First part is Awareness. Second part is Mind. Third part is Relationship. Fourth part is Habit. If parents read and attempt to implement all these parts well, it will be highly supportive for the kid's growth. When you as parents, read this book and relate it to your children, it might even work to clear some misunderstandings between parents and children, hence bridging the gap between your child and yourself. This book will even help you teach your children how to live harmoniously in society. This will help them behave and act responsibly not only at home, but also in the society.

Home, academic institutions and our society are the three platforms which support a child's development. Parents nowadays are raising their children by practicing consumer centric economics. Children are forgetting to play outside and are becoming excessively dependant on computers and mobile phones for entertainment and playing. Staying indoors for long periods of time, children are getting habituated to a luxurious and comfortable lifestyle. But, in spite of all the comforts and facilities, they are not able to express their happiness and feelings of joy as often as children of the past used to do. They have no idea how to share joy, friendship or love with siblings, friends and parents. We often forget that even children are miniature humans like us. Even they need respect and love from their elders. We often fail to value their individuality and the unique talents which each child possess.

Parents nowadays are insecure about exposing their children to failures. So, most children are oblivious to what failures are, and do not know anything about experiencing or dealing with setbacks in life. But instead, they must be demonstrated that failures are a part of life and they are to be faced bravely. Due to over-dependence on electronics, children, without realising the importance of relationships, are living as if living on a lone island. Most children do not realise the value of a good night's sleep. Staying up late in the night makes them devoid of a refreshing body and mind. Parents should give more priority to spending time with them rather than buying them expensive gifts and toys. Guiding a child towards a successful and accomplished path is the prime responsibility of every parent. I believe that this book will serve as a guideline for all those parents who sacrifice their life to provide their children with bright futures.

ALAN JOSEPH
MADURAI-625003
MOBILE: 8870795112
MAIL ID: alanjoseph.joseph96@gmail.com

PART - 1 (AWARENESS)

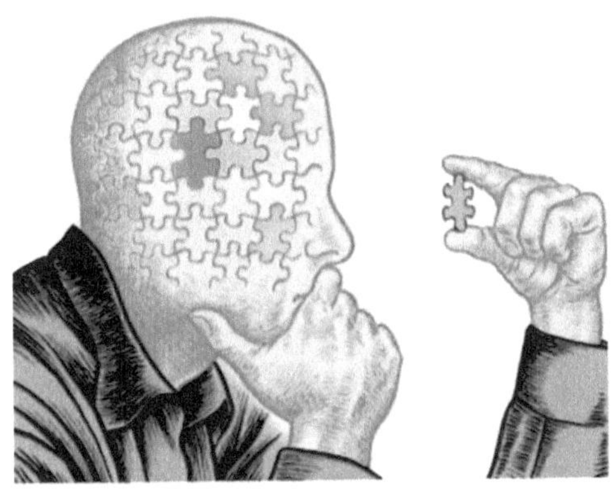

THE KNOWLEDGE OF ONE WHO DOES NOT KNOW HIS IGNORANCE, WILL DISTRACT HIM.---VETLY

CHAPTER ONE

UNDERSTANDING OF MENTAL HEALTH

The best medicine for mental illness is nothing but silence. ---- ARISTOTLE.

People's understanding of mental health and mental illness is low. We do not give much importance to or emphasise on mental health as much as we do on physical health. Hence, every year, more and more people are getting diagnosed with one or the other type of mental illness. The most common one is Depression. Depression is one of the most debilitating diseases of the world. Stress ranks fifth in the disease rankings. One's feelings, thought and behaviour, all three play an important role in the mental health of a person. It is not obviously seen to the naked eye, unlike wounds. In a human being, only if the body and mind work together, can the energy be utilised in the right direction.

Events:

Around 8 years ago, there were a family of three : a father, mother and their daughter. The girl was studying plus 2. She was adamant on not wanting to write the midterm examination. So, failing to convince her and being unable to cope up with the situation as the examination was fast approaching, they brought her to me. The father opined that they had provided more than the necessary facilities to their daughter. That is the reason she is denying to attend the examinations. The mother felt that she had been going to school against her wish and hasn't been studying sufficiently at all. However the daughter said that she has experienced a lot of failure since she finished her tenth grade. So she felt that whatever she had been doing wasn't right. She hadn't slept for days and had been experiencing constant fear in her mind. Being unable to make any decisions, she admitted trying to convey her situation to her parents. But, all she was being replied to was not to be afraid. They would encourage her to go to school fearlessly. So, she tried to relate the same thing to one of her teachers at school.

The teacher immediately called up her parents and discussed with them the need for a psychological counselling for their daughter. But, as things would have it, the parents became angry at the teacher and expressed their anger at her. They demanded if she was labelling their daughter as crazy. Thus, finding no solution to her problem, the girl totally shut herself down and stopped expressing her feelings to anyone at all. At that point of time, the parents had to decide about getting a psychiatric counselling done. So, they visited a family doctor and related the entire problem to him. Even the family doctor then referred them to a psychiatric counsellor.

QUESTIONS TO PONDER OVER FROM THE ABOVE EVENT:

i.   Was the need for parental counselling understood in the above mentioned situation?
ii. Why did the parents become angry on the teacher?
iii. Did the student want to be the 'perfect one'?

DESCRIPTION:

In our current society, mental counselling is seen as a disgrace. It is more like a stigma. Most of the times, even the parents are a factor in influencing a students' thoughts, feelings and actions. Like the parents described in the above event, many other parents choose to ignore the mental problems prevailing in their family. One of their several fears may be about the opinion of others, about them in the society. Becoming angry with the teacher can be explained by the lack of the ability for judgement, ignorance, inability to grasp the reality or even superstition. Some parents even think from the society's perspective about how others might react to them when they come to know about them opting for a psychological counselling. This kind of thought might also pose a barrier from reaching out to a psychiatric hospital.

Today's students aspire perfection. They would choose to be perfect rather than excelling and being the best. This creates an attitude that thirsts only for success. But this particular attitude leaves no room for being able to withstand failures. They do not know how to react to failures or loses. It is impossible for anyone to take only the correct decisions always and be successful. It is natural to make tiny mistakes and to take pitfalls for the same. Our success or failure in a particular situation is determined by a lot of factors. So it is important that when we face challenges, we need to think about both the sides of the coin.

When the student starts concealing her thoughts and stops expressing her feelings, her depression intensifies further. When the student attended the counselling sessions, her ability to endure the problems and her ways to deal with them were further explored. She was talked to and helped to explore her own feelings. The second aid was given to the parents about the psychology of these young students in general and about their daughter in particular and about why and how she needed help. After this, the student did attend her examination successfully and came out with flying colours.

THOUGHTS:

Superstitions about mental illness are prevalent in society. It is usually seen as a shame or stigma to reach out a psychiatrist or a counsellor. People tend to cover up when any of their family members show any signs and symptoms of any mental disorder. Most people are ignorant of the extent of seriousness of the illnesses. They sow false beliefs in their thoughts. Movies, newspapers and the way peers express their opinions about mental health all support their views about it as a social stigma. Many rumours about psychiatry are circulating in the society and on social media. These further add to the woes.

Mental illness is a disease similar to diabetes. It is caused by a chemical change in the brain. It is treatable with pills and efficient counselling. Pills however, do not cause addiction in this case. Some patients tend to discontinue their medication shortly after seeing a psychiatrist, citing that their problem has improved or has been solved. The pill should however be discontinued only on the doctor's advice. Otherwise, symptoms often tend to reappear. The doctor prescribes medication to every patient differently, depending on their nature of illness and the severity of their disorder. Patient should understand that as soon as the doctor sees signs of recovery, he will start tapering the dosage of the medication. By the time the patient makes a full recovery, the pills would have stopped. Most people however, do not understand this.

There are three major types of treatments for mental health disorders.

i. Counselling
ii. Psychotherapy
iii. Psychiatry

Counselling:
This aims at presenting the problem and helps in solutions for short term. There are laws and regulations regarding this in place. This is a much scientific practice

prevalent in these days.

Psychotherapy:

Disorders related to mental illness can present serious and difficult symptoms. This therapy works by making the patient recollect his past incomplete and unfinished desires or needs and using the same for a change of thought and action in the present. This helps the patient either forgive someone or something in his past and helps him make peace with it at present.

Psychiatry:

This kind of treatment focuses on treating symptoms caused by disorders like mental pressure, depression and suicide like thoughts. The treatment is extended according to the severity of the disorder. This treatment is ideal for patients who hurt self or affect family members negatively and in the process, tend to damage relationships unintentionally.

EXERCISES:

Tips for developing and improving mental health:

1. You should not think that everything that happens in life is taking place only with you. If you do not compare yourself with others, you will be able to take care of your own happiness, keep yourself enthusiastic and enhance your curiosity.

2. There is a saying, "the wise learn from their experiences.". You must use the experience you gathered from your life and your mistakes, to learn from them to build your future. Only then can you attain the mental boldness necessary to withstand failures in your future.

3. If you maintain an open mind, you would be able to give up your ego of 'I' or 'me'. This in turn will bring an

understanding between those around you and yourself. You would spread joy and love to those around you.

4. There may be some instances in your past which stick on to your mind like bitter memories. You should learn either to let go of the incident or to forgive the person because of whom the bitter memory was created. Holding on to it and reminiscing it will do no good ever.

5. You happen to experience many things in your everyday life for which you should be consciously thankful. If you practice thankfulness, you would exist in harmony with nature. Such coexistence will turn you into a grateful person.

6. Exercising for 15minutes daily will keep your body and mind healthy. You would be able to maintain a good mood all day.

7. If you practice distancing yourself from your electronic devices consciously, that itself will help in self-improvement.

8. A quality sleep is one of the many solutions which contributes to a refreshing mood. The amount of sleep necessary for an individual varies according to age. So maintaining the correct sleeping window is essential to maintain a good and refreshing mood and a relaxing feel.

9. Continue learning as long as you live. It expands your imagination, knowledge and your world. It also helps to connect with your people and recollect your memories as well.

10. Seeking help when you need it, is important for your path to a healthy growth.

CHAPTER TWO

DISCIPLINE AND ETHICS

GOOD QUALITIES ARE ABOVE GOOD LAWS. --- EDMUND BURKE.

Home is a place where good habits are taught and made to practice. As parents, we must allow our children to get creative and learn on their own. The experience of learning and the mistakes they make will pave way for them to the path of development. The duty of their parents is to lead their children in the right direction of life. Parents often like and appreciate their children to be disciplined. And only parents can create the situations that teach and encourage discipline in a young age.

EVENTS:

A few years ago, the parents of a second year student came along with her to meet me. They said that their son was adamant on changing the college in which he was studying in. But, his current college itself was the second college he had changed to recently. Because of this, they were facing several difficulties. The parents themselves opined that they did a mistake by not pointing out and correcting his mischief during his childhood. So, at present, he was behaving in an extremely indisciplined way and was being extravagantly disobedient.

To this, the student replied that he was facing lots of rules and regulations in his current college and he did not get experience the expected freedom. Hence, he felt that the college was unsuitable for him and he wanted to switch. He further revealed that he had changed 8 schools during his schooling period alone because he felt it difficult and challenging to accommodate to the rules imposed generally on all the students. So, the parents not knowing what to do, approached me.

QUESTIONS TO PONDER OVER FROM THIS EVENT:

1. Does the parents' upbringing seem to be the root of the problem?
2. Is it correct to expect discipline from a child without exercising discipline and rules at home and making sure that they were followed ?
3. Is the students' mind capable of accepting the rules and regulations exercised by the educational institutions or do they have a revolting mind-set in response to the rules? Is such freedom even necessary?
4. Did the student's expected independence take him on a path of self-development?

DESCRIPTION:

The basis of upbringing is discipline. And raising disciplined children in a single day or overnight is not possible. The same goes for a student. Since childhood, the parents could not convince or make the child follow discipline at home and he is free to behave the way he wants at home. Even when choosing a school for the child, they would choose one according to his choice, without restrictions. Being brought up like that, he expected his college to offer freedom like that at home. And when he did not get the expected freedom, he thought about changing schools and colleges.

This kind of upbringing results in the student not being mature enough to understand the parents' circumstance. He also suffers from a situation in which he cannot cross the luxury circle. He wants to continue the same way of life. Teaching discipline at an older age can be a daunting task. Some people, however, will get through the learning process of discipline with time. Many learn discipline through their own personal experiences.

Parents wanting to give their children a happy home and a comfortable school is not wrong. But, they should design a way to mix responsibility with the freedom and comforts. Home is the first place where good habits are taught. And school is a place where discipline and restrictions are exercised. Only if the rules are created and made to follow properly, an orderliness will prevail. This kind of atmosphere encourages the discipline.

It is not wrong to crave and experience freedom. In the same way, it is not wrong to reconsider that freedom if it is detrimental to others and us in a way that hinders growth. Freedom without rules and regulations does not lead us on the right path. Instead of growth, it might lead us to pitfalls.

Rules, regulations and discipline are the ways of our society. We have created them to lead a civilised life. However, being unable to accept the pressure of rules and discipline and not wanting to change himself, he would seek solace in changing schools and colleges, only expecting some institution to be of his choice. This is purely because of the student's habits.

We should be aware that with passing time, a habit gets modified and develops into discipline. Self-discipline is another form of orderly discipline which involves taking care of and valuing self a lot. It involves going through self-restraints. Those who practice self-discipline find it easier to protect themselves from impulses and influences.

The student was offered counselling on discipline according to his requirement and with the help of his parents. Then, after some consecutive years of counselling and follow up, he realised that self-discipline was created to help man take up responsibility efficiently. The student graduated from the same college with a Masters degree. Soon, he started working and was leading a responsible life.

THOUGHTS:

Children must be made to learn discipline from a tender age. Parents should model their upbringing i.e they should practice whatever they preach. Children learn by watching rather than by following instructions. If they want to raise disciplined children, they themselves should practice the same. Children even learn through experiences and observations.

If the child misbehaves, then beating or treating them with disrespect is not the way to go. You cannot expect them to listen to you when you are exasperated. Children are not going to learn discipline by punishment. Pointing out their mistakes with love can help modifying their line of thought. They look at us and learn more about discipline by the way we enact what we preach. We must be role models for our children. Child upbringing is an art because it takes a lot of patience to do that. Our attitude and the way we express our views and try to communicate to our children modifies their thoughts and helps us change ourselves too. When we come across any iconic rules or come to know of them from some sources, we could implement them at home to teach and model discipline.

Sometimes, it is good to let the children create the rules themselves. That way, they will learn to adhere by the rules made by them. It will even help them to learn being accountable for their actions. These are the rules followed by every society. It's a simple fact that if we practice discipline, sooner or later, our children will observe and will follow us.

Both children and adults need to understand that rules are looked upon differently by each one of them. Adults must follow their own rules and set an example. The rules teach self-control. Children cannot be made to understand the need to follow the rules. Even if you sit to teach the importance of rules, they would not understand and would brush it all away. Instead, the parents need to lower their expectations and make rules which are easily understandable and seem easy for kids to practice. This process happens slowly over a period of time, with love and care. Gradually, the children will like doing things in a certain way as they grow up.

Parents must practice something called 'tough love'. It is showering your children with love along with a pinch of strictness. This kind of things taught by parents to children will go far beyond academic education.

EXERCISES:

WAYS TO TEACH CHILDREN DISCIPLINE IN A GOOD WAY:

1. Share your thoughts with children in an open minded way. This will help maintain an intimacy with your children and will maintain the love and affection.
2. It is necessary to lovingly rebuke the mistakes made by children. However, punishing makes it impossible for the child to realise the mistake and change themselves
3. Just like a young bamboo can be bent easily, parents must start working on teaching discipline and inculcating values into children from a tender age.
4. Parents must be strict with the disciplined rules to be followed and the habits to be inculcated. They should even assist and encourage the children to implement the same.
5. The discipline learned and exercised at home will help them lead a smooth life ahead.
6. If kids help you do some small chores at home, it will give them a sense of self-respect and boost their self-esteem. They will even learn to be accountable for their own actions.
7. Share the new things you learn in your everyday life with your children, according to their age level.
8. Stay together with kids taking care of them and observing their little signs and feelings. This will enable you to understand them better.

9. Discipline, virtue and self-control are the three pillars essential for child upbringing.

10. Parents need to set example or model whatever they preach their child.

CHAPTER THREE

UNDERSTANDING THE CHANGE

WHEN WE EXPERIENCE A CHANGE, WE HATE IT AND LOVE IT AT THE SAME TIME. THIS IS OUR CONFUSION. WE EXPECT EVERYTHING TO BECOME BETTER WITHOUT CHANGE.

- SIDNEY G. HARRIS.

The only thing that doesn't change in life is CHANGE. The phenomenon of change can be described as a formation of a new leaf that eventually falls off the tree. The way the birth of the new leaf cannot be prevented, the falling of the leaf after sometime is inevitable. The benefits of growth and development can be experienced only if we bear a mind-set to accept the change which has happened. Our lives ought to be under own control. However, we must take note that we can be in charge of only some things in our lives. So, we should get used to complying things which cannot be controlled by us.

EVENTS:

There was a family. The father was a policeman and the mother took care of everyone and everything around. She was the homemaker. They had a child after around 15years of marriage. Naturally, the child was brought up with extreme love and protection. The child was brought up in an extremely safe environment and was nurtured by being provided all the possible facilities. They would see to it that the child never faced any hardship. If the child adamantly demanded anything, the father would instantly buy it. In some instances, when the child does not listen to the parents, the situation would escalate into a heated argument and it would turn out to be an annoying situation for both of them. Since the early age of the child to the present day, no decision has ever been made in the family wholeheartedly by the parents and the son together.

The parents wanted to bring up their child with the values and the ways of life which they had learned and experienced over their lifetime. But, their son being of the current generation and him constantly observing his surroundings, could not understand and implement his parents' ways and instructions. So, the parents and their son could never reach a compromised point for making any decision together as a family. Now that he had reached the 8th grade, the parents were confused about his behaviour and did not know how to handle his ways. So, they approached me for some guidance or clarity regarding how to manage their adolescent son.

QUESTIONS WE HAVE TO PONDER UPON FROM THE EVENTS:

1. Is there a difference between the knowledge from experience, statement of the parents' and the child's current mind-set?
2. The child, having been raised in an extremely safe environment with all the facilities, does he bear the courage necessary to face change in his life?

DESCRIPTION:

The parents have a lot of practical knowledge accumulated over a period of time by their own experience. On the other hand, the son had the detailed knowledge which comes by observation, naturally, in this generation. Thus, the way he learned things was different. The way people learn things in each generation has been and will be different. It is not wrong wanting to give comfortable lifestyle to our children. However, allowing them to be in that state of comfort all the time is wrong. The parents should let the children know about the hardships and sufferings they faced. The children should have the chance to realise that life is really challenging at times. The parents must show the children about their current hardships they are facing to live their current lifestyle.

In reference to the above mentioned event, because of the hardships faced by the parents, they did not wish their son to go through the same and hence provided him a comfortable lifestyle. So now, when he is not obeying his parents, becoming endlessly angry on them and is not able to accept changes which come naturally with age, they are becoming anxious.

As a remedy, the parents were taken for counselling sessions regarding how to deal with teenagers and their nuances. Then, the student was provided counselling on responsibility, self-regulation, the need to respect others and how to deal with anger. He made good progress. Now, they live together as a happy family. The son has reached 11th grade and is doing well in life.

The world is undergoing changes every minute. This is natural and inevitable. Any new situation naturally causes some kind of fear and anxiety. Ignoring these or pushing them aside is equal to refusing to enjoy the pleasures of life. If you want to do good to your children, expose them to hardships. Allow them to experience difficulties. Let us teach them to swim through the sea of life and sing simultaneously. Let us practice tough love.

THOUGHTS:

Life is an anthology of changes which occur naturally and a collection of events which are inevitable and are eventually destined to happen. Change is the only thing that does not change. The difference between generations is evolution of technology and the growth of knowledge in all fields simultaneously. In the same way, children's growth patterns, functional habits, and situational development all changes simultaneously with time. This is the XYZ generation gap as stated by a research. To understand the current generation Z and to understand the gap between the XY generation and the Z generation, this research articles is useful. By knowing the birth year of each generation, we can determine which generation we belong to.

- Silent generation – 1900 to 1945
- Baby boomers – 1946 to 1964
- X generation – 1965 to 1980
- Y generation – 1981 to 19956
- Z generation – 1996 to till date

DETAILS OF THE Z GENERATION:

The Z generation is said to be the electronic device generation. This generation started from 1996 till date. By age, everyone between 7 to 22 years old, belong to this generation. This generation has enhanced technological skills and is also called Social Networking Generation. They exchange information mostly via social networking sites.

91% YouTube, 75% WhatsApp, 66% Snapchat, 65% Instagram and 71% Facebook. The sites which they watch crazily are Google, Netflix, Facebook, YouTube, Tiktok, and Amazon's prime. So, this generation encounters various kind of problems like bullying (online and offline), not being interested in studies, various mental disorders like depression, anxiety, suicidal thoughts ,emotional imbalance, technology addiction, drink and drug addiction and health disorders like malnutrition insomnia and eye problems.

The following are some of the research articles and journals published about Z Generation.

The Z generation uses five different social channels a day. 75% watch videos on YouTube every week. At least 44% of the Z gen visit social media at least once in 15 minutes. One in five people spend more time posting and updating themselves on new things, rather than just reading and looking at social media, such as Twitter, Instagram, Facebook and TikTok. 42% of them, however, report that social media does affect their self- esteem.

X , Y , Z Generation - Overview			
Profile / Characteristics	Generation X	Generation Y	Generation Z
Born in	1965 – 1980	1981 – 1995	1996 – still
Age group	39 to 54	23 to 38	7 to 22
Technology	VCR, Walkman	Internet, Email, SMS	iPad, Facebook, Android
Influencers	Practitioners	Experienced peers	User-generated forums
Learning format	Spontaneous & interactive	Multi-sensory & Visual	Student-centric Kinesthetic
Learning environment	Round-table style relaxed ambience	Safe-style with music & multi -modal	Lounge room style multi-stimulus
Financial values	Medium-term goals credit savvy	Short-term wants credit dependent	Impulse purchases e-stores
Training focus	Practical, case studies, applications	Emotional, stories, participative	Multi-model, eLearning, interactive
Aspiration	Work-life balance	Freedom and flexibility	Security and stability
Signature product	Personal computer	Smart phone	Nano-computing, 3-D print, driverless cars
Communication media	E-mail and SMS	SMS or Social Media	Hand-held communication devices

The table above gives an understanding of the details and characteristics of each generation. It can be understood that Z generation people have very different ways of learning and their activities too are very different from those of the other generations.

Here are some ways parents can handle Z – generation children:

- Get to know your kid's friend circle.
- Keep an eye on the type of electronic devices used by children. Coordinate their necessity and organise their screen time appropriately. They should be allowed to watch things which might be useful to them.
- Teach them the value of human interaction. Allow them to meet people around you and get to know each of them gradually.
- Use parental controls for different apps which are installed on your devices. This will help you to monitor their screen time and to regulate the source of the technology which they are observing and learning.

- Use the three W rule of Where When and Who. It is about where children learn to think and act. When do they act? Who do they idolise?
- Respect the privacy of children. But this does not mean that covert behaviour or seemingly strange activities would be acceptable. Such actions are to be questioned.
- Try to involve children in outdoor activities like sports or in arts or crafts. Once they get a hang of such things, they themselves will stay away from useless browsing or will use electronic devices for useful activities and learning.

Now, let's see how to make the best use of all the technological advancement and how to deal with the unwanted.

The fact that life becomes easier if you're accustomed to accepting changes, does not change. Striving to learn and engage ourselves in the new developments will help us reach a new stage of self-development.

For example, if you are used to drinking coffee and one morning, you suddenly run out of it, then you might want to have some tea for that day. Take the alternative.

If you are on the way to your workplace, try taking an alternate route for a day or two or 3 times a month. Getting to know of different routes might help you take the alternate route in case of a traffic jam or congestion.

Look back to several hundreds of years ago. Compare with the present. Change is evident in all the fields. And still lot of changes are taking place every minute. New industries with renewed concepts are emerging and replacing the older technologies. The newer industries are striving to suit the new times and meet the demands of the current growing generation. Technology and internet play an important role in this.

Take the entertainment industry for example. Once upon a time there was no television at all. Radio got invented and it created a revolution in the market. After some years, came television. People were fascinated by the concept of watching the small box. Gradually, the radio then got outdated. Then, the Internet was invented just at the time when I thought that there were no new inventions to be made and changed everything around us with a bang. Amazon prime, Netflix, YouTube, Hotstar, et cetera, all these applications embraced the change. I opine that the online website channels will pose great challenges to the daily television channels in the years to come.

The advancements brought about by technology transcends various sectors and ultimately has the greatest impact on the individual, home, community, cultures, education and industries. As stated in the research papers, X, Y and Z generations and the generation gap, new changes are taking place in this world as each generation enters into a new phase. It might be a little too much for us to grasp all of this at present. But the ever developing technology doesn't wait for anyone.

Children hold the capacity to absorb the changes fast and this will be evident to the parents who are keenly observing their child's activities. Their expressions, speech, behaviour and even personality shows a bit of change. Weather we want to approach children according to their generational pattern or trying to change children in your generational perspective and experience, if the children grow up to be disciplined, organised and socially relevant individuals, all our attempts would be worthwhile. It is our perspective and approach that teaches children the attitude of accepting change.

EXERCISES:
How to teach the quality of accepting change:

1. Teach children coping skills through identifying their strengths rather than challenging the new changes around them.
2. Teach your children the difference between courage and responsibility. They should be explained that courage is not the absence of fear, but, it is the ability to face fear.
3. Encourage children to think and act independently. Try to increase their self-confidence when they try to do things on their own and complimenting them on achieving small milestones.
4. Sharing your success stories and failures with children will help them understand and build patience and forbearance. It will also inculcate the attitude of accepting.
5. Try to show children the various new events happening in your life and surroundings. They will learn to prepare themselves for situations like dealing with strangers or new circumstances.
6. Try to be concerned and supportive of them when they deal with setbacks and disappointment.
7. In children, fear turns into anxiety within no time. Help your child cope with fear before they start having anxiety issues.
8. Encourage humour. Let them realise the value of humour and happiness. Laughter is a great medicine (only if its motives are good).
9. Give children the opportunity to make their own decisions in their everyday life. This will help them develop the ability to make meaningful resolutions.

10. Teach children that we cannot control everything that happens around us. They should be taught how to handle inevitable events with the mind-set to accept them.

• 26 •

PART - 2 (MIND)

If you want to know someone's mind, listen to the words he speaks.—— Chinese proverb

CHILDHOOD INNER WOUNDS AND IMPRINTS

Out of all the qualities of a person like richness, intellect, value, and being respectable, the best one is being benevolent.

- Henry Ward Beecher.

Children's minds are like white pages, pure and innocent. The everyday events, television, words spoken by people around, and the daily experiences, all account for forming memories and are remembered by a child's mind. The events which occur before 3 years of age of a child are imprinted on the subconscious mind. They shape up the child's thoughts, feelings and behaviour, which become apparent, only later in life.

EVENTS:

There was a fourth grader at school. She was a naughty kid, like most kids her age. She had a younger brother. They both would play together as often as they would fight. Sometimes, the girl would be scolded or punished by her mother for being quite a prankster. At her home, her parents would often have heated arguments and fights. At those times, she would stay by her mom's side at home.

Once a week, her school teacher would communicate with the parents to detail them about her behaviour at school. To this, the parents would reply that they have been reprimanding the child at home.

One day at school, when she was playing on the field with her friends, a fight ensued and they beat each other. Then, when she came to the class with that bitter experience in her mind, she suddenly became angry while the teacher was taking class. She jabbed a pencil into the back of the child sitting in front of her. The poor child started wailing as she was in pain and was bleeding profusely. Unfortunately, the pencil went deep and it's tip broke inside her body.

The shocked teacher immediately called the nurse, got first aid done and informed her parents' over phone. The headmistress summoned her parents, and strongly condemning the act, recommended psychological counselling sessions for her. She asked them to visit the school again after a week. The distressed parents then met me with their child.

QUESTIONS TO PONDER OVER FROM THIS EVENT:

1. Does parental squabbles and arguments affect the child's mood and behaviour?
2. Did the child enact the way she observed things at home, between her parents?
3. Is the child unknowingly exposing her innermost subconscious feelings, which she could never express otherwise?

DESCRIPTION:

Condemning a mistake is different from mental punishment. Condemning is pointing out his mistake and explaining him about it, so that he realises his misdoings and willingly acts upon correcting it. On the other hand, punishment is what we do by word and deed. It is focused on correcting the person rather than correcting the mistake. We often resort to scolding or spanking. I opine that if we pay attention to the correcting the mistake, the child will eventually understand and will get better. However, if we are bent upon trying to straighten the child out, then the problem is likely to manifest itself in one way or the other, again. When the child committed the mistake, then and there, I understood that this was the case. We should not force our ideas and intellect on the child. Rather, we should get down to the child's level of understanding for him/her to follow creed. The solution to a problem lies in how you decide to face the problem and to deal with it.

In the initial days, a mother is everything to the child. The father, brothers, sisters, schoolmates, relatives etc get involved into the child's life only later. The behaviour patterns of the mother affects the child mentally later in life. It would be wrong on the parents' part if they try to put excessive restrictions beyond the understanding capacity of the child. Expectations that exceed the child's abilities and conflicts between the parents in teaching morals etc. affect the child's line of thought and personality.

If parents are always loggerheads or are separated, the child will be affected emotionally. Children observe everything around them. The words which are uttered during the fights between parents are subconsciously noted and remembered by the children. Knowingly or unknowingly, they utter the same words in schools or at any other places. A child cannot differentiate between the good and the bad. He just absorbs everything said and done from the surroundings and parents. Children notice everything that happens at home, notice everything that is talked about and collects all the information into his mind. The child learns whatever he/she is exposed to. Whatever the child learns, the parents are solely responsible.

After all, getting involved into brawls at home and in the neighbourhood is a way for the children to express their anger. If children are reprimanded harshly, the feelings accumulated thus, in a course of several days could be exhibited at school in the form of conflict with friends.

Later, through several sessions like Art therapy and Play therapy , the child was made to talk about her problems and the negative emotions lurking in her mind. She was given counselling on how to deal with those emotions.

Later, the parents were given counselling over multiple sessions. They were explained the need to be role models for the development and growth of the child. Today, the child is in 7th grade. She willingly exhibits her best behaviour at home and school. She has been a class leader and guides the other students in her class.

THOUGHTS:

The foetus is made up of genetic records from both the mother and the father. The mental development of the child starts as early as during pregnancy and after birth. The baby naturally has a strong sense of attraction towards the parents, the prime people who nurture the child. This bond strengthens with time as the baby is fed and cared for. There forms a loving and harmonious relation between them. Gradually, over time, the baby's mind, being as blank as a white sheet of paper, imbibes the personality of the parents. As the child grows, he gets accustomed to the community around him, experiences various emotions and circumstances and likes to play with friends. He gets various opportunities to bond with people around him. This helps him become a socially active being and builds self-confidence. Family plays an important role in the development of the child's personality. Children observe how we face our everyday problems and learn watching it. Only in some situations, does the child reveal whatever he had been learning subconsciously. The events would have been embedded in the mind of the child. Since the baby mind has no barriers, they express themselves without any judgement of good and bad. All his observations have been ingrained in his mind while growing up

According to psychologists, by the time the child is 3years of age, the brain develops almost completely. Even psychologically, his feelings and moods surface out. There is a prominent difference in the way children and adults process information. The daily routine events is keenly observed and will be directly embedded in children mind. That's because there is no barrier in a child's mind. So they expose whatever is there in their mind without judging if it is good or bad.

But the other family members are emotionally experienced individuals. This experience acts as a barrier when they face the same circumstances. That filter acts according to the personality and development of each person. The events surrounding the person and his experiences are all filtered before becoming a part of his memories. This is the fundamental thing on which our life is based. Depending on the circumstances faced by an individual, his personality is revealed and developed simultaneously.

EXERCISES:

WAYS TO NURTURE CHILDREN WITH GOOD NATURE AND LOVE:

1. The basic need of every child is love. Though it is the natural duty of every parent to make the child feel loved, for some parents around the world, this has been quite challenging.
2. Parents should not try to control their children. They should be given freedom and should be raised with self-confidence. They should be taught living in harmony with social principles.

3. Children should be taught the importance of treating others respectfully. Only then, will others be able to reciprocate them. Encourage yourself to love others. Only then, others can treat you the same way.

4. Encourage children to be responsible in the same way you are.

5. Share your life's successes and failures with your children.

6. Express your love, care and concern to your children in a way understandable by them.

7. Expose your children to various people in the society and let them know about the various social norms. This will upscale their social skills. This further will help them deal with various situations later on, in life.

8. Spend a lot of time with your children and gain their confidence. They must be able to confide in you and share whatever is there on their mind with you.

9. When the children talk to you, or are sharing some thoughts with you, do not interrupt them. When they have completed whatever they wanted to say, you can express your appreciation or an alternative feedback to them.

10. When communicating with your child, talk to them by holding their hand or patting their back. This will help strengthen the bond between your kid and you.

CHAPTER FIVE

CONNECTION BETWEEN FEAR AND SECURITY

YOU CAN ELEVATE THE WORLD IF YOU CHANGE YOUR MIND. - NORMAN VINCENT PEEL.

Fear is a feeling which haunts man and manifests itself through health. Fear hampers with our attempts at things. It prevents us from activating our energies and our talents, limiting us into a compact circle. It interferes with showing out our confidence and taking a step forward. Three things possibly happen due to fear: One is running away from fear. Second is freezing out of fear and third is facing the fear and struggling to get over it.

EVENTS:

In a family, the father is working at IT sector. The mother is the homemaker, taking care of everything at home. They have 2 children, both studying at the same school. The son is in 3rd standard and the daughter was in 1st standard. The daughter was good at studies. But, in the recent days, she would start crying adamantly about not wanting to go to school. Just before starting to school, she would weep saying she wouldn't go and wanted to stay at home with her mother. In case of missing the school bus in all this chaos, either of the parents would take the responsibility of dropping her at school.

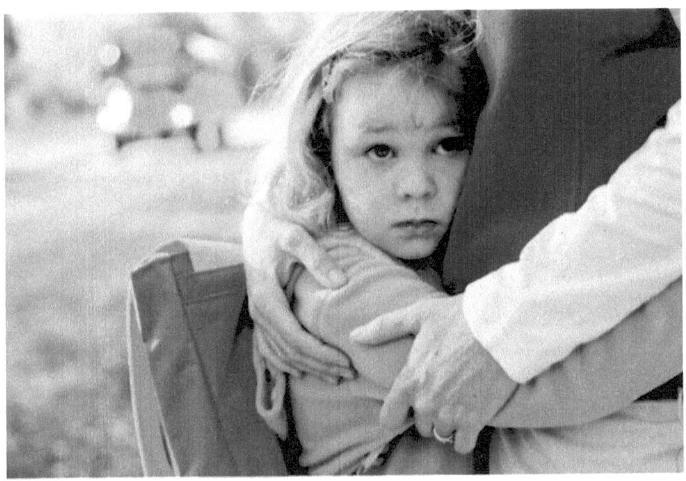

The girl even tried to jump off the school gate and run away several times. Even at school, sometimes she would tearfully demand going home. Once when she was trying to run away from classes, and her teacher tried to restrain her by holding her hand, she bit and scratched her in an attempt to free herself. During interval, she would prefer sitting in her brothers' class room with him. Because of such difficult behaviour, her teachers couldn't concentrate on the other students.

So they took this matter to the assistant HM. So, the assistant HM summoned the parents and questioned them about her behavioural patterns at home. The parents answered that she had been adamant about not wanting to go to school and would insist on going the day after. She would shriek and create a big hue and cry. They were in a fix, not knowing what to do. So, the HM suggested the need of a psychiatrist. They were assured not to worry about her studies as she was a brilliant student. She would learn things quickly. "If you need any help from our school, we will do it willingly." Saying this, the HM urged them to consult a psychiatrist. So, the parents had come to meet me with their child regarding the same.

QUESTIONS TO PONDER OVER FROM THIS EVENT:

1. What is the reason for the child preferring to sit in her brother's classroom?
2. What is the reason for the child to be adamant on running from the classroom and biting and hurting her teacher?
3. When the girl was adamant on not wanting to go to school, why were the parents not concerned about the cause of such behaviour?

DESCRIPTION:

The cause of fear in children is insecurity. When she was in LKG and UKG, her classes were being conducted in a separate building in school. Their class had just two teachers. But from the 1st standard, she had to attend classes in a bigger building, in the same school. The change from the smaller building to a bigger building and encountering different teachers for each of the subjects made her nervous. Each teacher had a different approach to the students and the subject. The child could not comprehend this difference and could not accept the change. Hence she wanted to avoid going to school altogether.

Even before she prepared herself for the switch, she had to face another change. This created a lot of confusion in her mind and mixed feelings of fear and insecurity became a blockade for her to go to school. Other children in the class had a firm belief that they have support from other people like teachers and staff around. That's how they faced their insecurities. A feeling of fear is natural when facing a change or a new situation. Children who are attached to people around them tend to experience less fear and anxiety. Such children will be able to solve problems efficiently. This is exactly what is called social and emotional development of children.

When her classes started to take place in the new building, being in her brother's classroom with him in the recess period, gave her a sense of security. So, she would do the same thing every day to comfort herself. When her teacher restrained her from running away from classes, not knowing what to do, she bit and scratched her teacher out of fear. In my opinion, this kind of situation is caused by lack of social a exposure and development. She never communicated with her fellow students. She never got used to playing with other children. So when encountering new changes, she couldn't face it. She took longer than other children just to accept the changes.

Initially, when the kid did not want to go to school, the parents shouldn't have neglected her behaviour and should have shown some concern. They should have examined the reason for her behaviour and should have scrutinised furthur at her school. If that had been done, then perhaps, her feelings of hatred for school and anger over her teachers could have been avoided. Maybe, even the mental confusion which was experienced by teachers and others at school could have been avoided.

In the sessions with the counsellor, the parents were guided on how to make children feel secured, how to win their confidence and how to install self confidence in the child's mind.

Then the child was given counselling sessions via play and drawing. The child was made to do practice courage through some exercises. Through these sessions and with the help of her school, teachers and parents, the counsellor tried his best to inculcate the virtue of boldness and courage into her mind. The child has showed good improvement in her mannerisms and attitude. She is now in 3rd standard.

THOUGHTS:

Fear is a feeling which oppresses and controls a person. Fear creates confusion in mind and makes us feel weak. It is a dreadful feeling which creates endless obstacles in our endeavours. Fear manifests in various ways. For eg. Fear of Examination, fear of heights , fear of endeavours, fear of failure, fear of separation, fear of loss, fear of future and countless such things.

It is a unique feeling which creates a driving force or a motivation in you, which may be either negative or positive. If you direct this motivational force in a positive way, it helps you develop new strategies to protect self, progress in life and create a new position for yourself. If the intensity of fear is high in you, it will generate tension and nervousness affecting our daily life. If fear is low, it causes reluctance, lack of interest in doing things, not making efforts or not involving into events.

There is a difference between fear and anxiety. Fear can influence you positively and you can grow to new heights in life. But, if the same fear affects you negatively, it becomes a barrier in your growth story. Excessive fear evokes tension and nervousness. Anxiety induced by fear can frustrate you enough to lose your temper. In such cases, your positivity and feelings of love can change to hatred. Fear would manifest in a small way, but the after effects of it could be huge. Anxiety can be considered as a symptom for mental illness and depression. Fear reveals insecurity from a psychological point of view. When children grow up without a sense of security, they fear almost everything in life. If a person feels secure and reliable in his life, all his fears will collapse. People search for security in various things. Some people search for it in money, some in building a home, some in securing a job, some in going for higher studies, some in gaining a position or status, some in living a rich life, and so on. But, none of all these things can give u a feel of complete security. A genuinely complete sense of security comes from self-confidence and in being able to confide in others. But, trying to search for reliability and security in superstitions is sheer foolishness.

EXERCISES:
HOW TO ALLEVIATE YOUR FEARS:

1. Try to know the root cause of the fear occurring within you and try to decipher the changes it is bringing in you.
2. Try practising Pranayama or Breathing Exercises. This relaxes the mind and other organs. Just by practising pranayama for at least 30mins a day, you'll experience an emotional tranquility.
3. Try maintaining a personal journal. Write down about your feelings when you experience fear. Think about the effects of fear on yourself and try to analyse the cause of it. Writing it all down presents a possibility of change of thought.

4. Learn to talk to yourself. Practice talking to self. Say to yourself," I'm brave and courageous." Repeat this at least 25 times before going to bed and when you wake up. This will strengthen you mentally.

5. If you are afraid of something, try visualising it in a good way. Do this as often as possible. This will help you get rid of the fearful emotions associated with that particular thing in your mind.

6. Start challenging your negative thoughts. Begin to look at it with a rational thinking and perspective.

7. When you experience fear and anxiety, your whole focus shifts only to that particular feeling. Try diverting your thoughts to good things in life, such as engaging in physical activity such as sports or engaging in some hobbies. This can help alleviate your anxiety gradually.

8. When making new beginnings, try doing so with an open mind. This will help you achieve the attitude of accepting the things that life throws at you.

9. Take a pause and give rest to your body and mind. As you rest, you can relieve yourself of the stress caused by fear. Even the symptoms of stress can regress by practising this.

10. For a person who suffers from excessive fear and loses his/her self awareness, it is strongly recommended to consult a psychiatrist or a counsellor and seek help.

CHAPTER SIX

UNDERSTAND THE VALUE OF OTHERS AND RESPECT IT

Everything we dispose isn't a waste. Each has a value of its own. —ANDY WARHAY HALL

Humans connect to each other via Trust. You honour a person based on how much you trust him. Trust is a feeling which acts as a bridge between parents and children. This is the exact feeling which acts as the strength of the parents in their relationship with their children. If your behaviour and attitude wins the trust of your children, they will show astounding growth and extraordinary development. But, nowadays, the value and love we express towards our children is directly proportional to their academic score. When children do mistakes, we ought to correct them. But instead if we use demeaning and abusive words and underestimate them, they will lose their self-esteem and self-confidence.

EVENTS:

In a home, there lived two boys with their parents and grandparents. Both of them studied in the same school. The elder one was in +2 and younger one was in 10th. They weren't quite close. The sibling bond between them was quite weak.

The younger son would not talk to anyone in school and was quite submissive by nature. Even his academic performance was just average. His class teacher would call their parents once a week and update·them about their son's academics and general behaviour at school. After some months, the parents met the teacher at the PTA meeting. The teacher showed them their son's quarterly examination answer sheet. The younger son had got less than 10 marks in each of the subjects. The teacher informed the parents that if his academic performance continued this way, he would not be allowed to take the public examination. Hearing this, the distressed parents came home with a heavy heart. Later, when the parents came to meet me, they related all these events in a short and concise way.

Of late, when the younger son went out, to school or even to some place around his home, he would avoid making eye contact with people while talking. He would just bend his head or look away while talking. Even though the parents knew this, they did not take it seriously. The mother did not ever raise this issue either, fearing that it would anger her son.

The parents would focus on him and his academics only during exam time and compel him to study. During the other days, he would study by himself. Since his childhood, his grandfather was the only person who would be his emotional support. Even if he did a small mistake, everyone else would storm out at him saying that he was a good for nothing and other such abusive words. Sometimes, based on the marks he got, he would be made fun of and commented upon at home. His mother would compare him to his older brother, speaking high of him. In such times, his grandfather would take his side and would comfort him.

But, as things would have it, the grandfather expired because of ill health. However, at that point of time, the younger one didn't cry at all. Not being able to come to terms with the fact that his grandfather is no more, he swallowed his grief and suppressed his feelings.

After some days, when he was studying being assisted by his mother, she asked him," How many times are you going to study the same topic like a stupid fool?" Hearing that, suddenly he burst with anger and beat up his mother. Further, he went around the house wildly breaking things. In such a situation, the parents came to meet me.

QUESTIONS TO PONDER UPON FROM THE ABOVE EVENTS:

1. Who were the people at home hindering the growth of the child's self-esteem?
2. What is the reason the son attack his mother?
3. What is the cause of the negative thoughts occurring in the boy's mind?

DESCRIPTION:

The reasons of the lack of self-esteem in the boy are countless. The father not showing enough concern for the child, the mother's attitude, her manner of expression and the words used by her are some of the reasons. The inability to accept the loss of his grandfather, the family system, lack of sleep and failing to trust parents are all obstacles to the boy's self-esteem. With so many problems weighing on, in his mind, he gradually lost confidence in himself so much so, that he couldn't even make eye contact when talking with people. Walking with a bowed head in a bid to avoid people, this feeling gradually got ingrained into his personality. This led to mood swings and physical changes during his adolescence.

Since he was carrying the weight of some unfinished events of his past, feelings like anger, hatred, anxiety and sadness overwhelmed him. The word 'stupid' said by his mother was always ringing in his ears and boggled his mind.

When his feelings clocked up together, his brain failed to make proper judgement of behaviour. The outburst caused him to attack his mother and break things in his home.

Even though the parents brought up their children with the same sense of affection, them comparing the younger one with the elder one caused him to be shameful of himself. Parents showing their affection based on his academic score hurt him extremely. These feelings, over a period of years have become ingrained in his mind and have led to a negative mood. The situations he faced at home, at school and the events around him, had all given him a hard time. Hence, his mind could develop only negative thoughts based on all those experiences.

As a solution, at first, the parents were given counselling in several sessions. They were enlightened about using appropriate words for children, working on their attitude towards their children and creating better family situations. As a result of the parents' changed attitude, they could observe small behavioural changes in the boy. During the several sessions with the boy, they tried approaching him through his negatively imprinted events, thoughts and feelings. During the counselling and psychotherapy sessions, a lot of details in his body language emerged, which needed to be comforted and corrected.

The result of the counselling sessions was clearly evident by his academic score. It improved considerably, just as his teachers and parents had expected. He scored 395 marks in his public examination. He is now studying in 11th standard.

THOUGHTS:

In today's consumerism based culture, the meaning of values keep changing. Until recently, it was considered prestigious to live frugally. But today, living frugally is considered not knowing how to enjoy life. In the past, traditionally, clothes were meant to cover our body decently. But today, clothes are used as a means to impress others. Dressing up scantily has become a norm. Until recent times, discipline was considered more of a virtue compared to academics. But today, people prioritise academic scores over manners and discipline. According to most people today, marks are more important, discipline will follow anyways. In the past, being affectionate, kind and disciplined was considered ideal. But, today, idols are those who speak fluent English and are rich. Most parents flaunt such people as examples to their children. Such people are introduced to children as great idols, whom they must follow.

Even when children grow in good cultural background, their innate childishness remains the same. We should not try to modify the children's abilities according to our understanding and comfort. Trying to guide them according their own talent would be a wise thing to do. For example, bullying and intimidating children for their mistakes will do good to neither of you. Rather, this affects the children in a bad way. This takes quite a toll on the self-confidence and the self-esteem of the child. It's just like pouring hot water to a plant.

By respecting our children and listening to what they have to say, you help build their self-esteem. Instead of punishing and insulting the child, their mistake should be verbally condemned and explained in a way they can understand. Most barents however resort to punishment to reform their child. According to a psychiatrist, the children who are feel insulted, tend to harbour feelings like anger, hatred, vengeance and intolerance quite aggressively. However, condemning and punishing becomes a necessary sometimes. But that depends on the way the situation is handled. Encouraging children to behave appropriately is a must. Your appreciation of their endeavours gives them a long lasting firm feel of self-confidence. Such children can boldly embrace the changes in their lives.

EXERCISES:

HOW TO BRING UP CHILDREN WHO UNDERSTAND THEIR OWN VALUE:

1. Talk to children affectionately and optimistically. Do not talk to them in a pessimistic or negative way.

2. Kids always expect you to talk a lot to them. They are always eager to express things and learn new things from you. Try to make small conversations with your children. This will create a strong relationship between them and yourself.

3. Do not scold harshly or treat them with disrespect in front of others. Doing so will strip them off their own self-respect.

4. When kids behave well or do good things, appreciate them immediately. Shower them with encouraging words.

5. Children yearn for your physical warmth. When you hold them closely, they feel secure. Children who are brought up lovingly have high levels of self-esteem.

6. When you play with your child, sometimes you should allow them to win. Feeling like a winner boosts their self-esteem. Little victories like this helps them confide in themselves.

7. Involve your children into discussions about issues concerning them. Try to listen to what they have to say and respect their opinions. This will make them feel important.

8. Let children take small decisions. When taking them out, allow them to purchase something and then ask them to write an account of the expenditure. This will enhance their decision making abilities and ways to handle money. This will be their initial lessons of financial management.

9. Encouraging children from time to time will illuminate their life.

10. Children should be given the new experience of interacting with people, making new friends, and communicating with people of different backgrounds. This will give them an opportunity to develop their social skills.

CHAPTER SEVEN

KNOWING AND DOING

The feeling of gratitude is a lot like your muscles. The more you use it, the more strength it gains. - Alan Cohen.

Qualities like personality, character, interests, habits and devotion are developed during childhood. Knowledge acquired during childhood stays with you for long. Family, parents and community, all play an important role in the growth of a child. In today's economic condition, both the parents must work and earn to meet their needs. Both children and adults are trying to adopt new habits according to their schedules for their own development. Even though they each know what to do, when doing it practically, the implementation doesn't go anywhere near to their knowledge.

EVENTS:

There was a family of three. Both the parents were doctors by profession. They had a daughter studying in 8th class. But, for some reason, she began being irregular at completing her homework soon after her 8th grade. She would not even concentrate during the class hours at school. She started scoring low marks in her examinations. So, her class teacher thought of updating her parents about her academic performance. But then, with the PTA meeting approaching the next week she planned to do it during the meeting.

At the PTA meeting, the teacher asked the child why her parents didn't turn up. She started to cry and replied," They were fighting with each other. So they asked me to go by myself. No one talks to me happily. I don't want to go home." To this the teacher consoled her that she should not say that way and that she would talk to her parents. She assured the child and sent her home. After a week, she summoned the child's parents and informed them about the condition of their daughter. As their daughter's teacher, she suggested them to consult a psychologist for the problems they are facing and for the sake of their daughter's future. She also requested the parents to forgive her if she was wrong.

In such a situation, the parents came to me. During a simple conversation with them, I inferred that it's been almost 5 years since they spoke to each other. Both of them were not ready to ask forgiveness to each other. Their demeanour clearly indicated this. At home, they were communicating with each other or passing messages to each other through their daughter. Owing to their ego, they held themselves to be correct in any kind of situation and it has been the same way since years. This state of their mind combined with their memories over a period of time, scarred their mind. They reminiscence on their scars constantly, are relate the same to their everyday events. This way, they couldn't ever give up on their bitterness. They wanted to forsake their egos for the sake of their daughter. But, when the mind wants to forgive, their intellect reminds them of the bitterness again. Hence, they are not able to do that. But, they needed to take this opportunity to forgive each other and lead a good family life.

QUESTIONS TO PONDER OVER FROM THE ABOVE EVENTS:

1. What is the barrier between the couple which prevents them from forgiving each other?
2. How intense is the psychological trauma caused by the parents' actions to their daughter?

DESCRIPTION:

Forgiveness is a virtue which may be easier to practice if asked for wholeheartedly. But, usually, it is never easy to ask for forgiveness or to forgive someone wholeheartedly. By apologising, even huge problems can crumble down to peace. However, nowadays, due to arrogance and lack of understanding, the sanctity of the virtue of forgiveness is disappearing. Even after realising their mistake, most people do not admit it because of selfishness and arrogance prevailing their mind. Be it a close friend, a relative, girlfriend, boyfriend, husband or wife, the interest which they show in proving themselves right in an argument, won't be there for apologising and accept mistakes. Ego was the main barrier between the couple to accept their mistakes. Stubbornness and being thankless could be the other reasons for not being able to forgive each other. Whatever be the reason, their conflict had wounded their daughter's mind severely. Because of their disputes, they could not express their love towards their daughter appropriately. They failed to understand the child's feelings and would often push her away when she wanted to have a conversation with them. Hence, as her happiness faded away, her academic grades too dropped.

They got so engrossed in their own problems and squabbles that they completely neglected about their daughter's future. They started to work for longer hours to get over their disturbed mind and feelings. Instead of being concerned and spending time with their child, they appointed a nanny to take care of her. This widened the gap between the parents and their child. Their mutual problems blindfolded their eyes so much so, that instead of finding a solution to their problem, they have been drowning into their own problems.

The couple opted for family counselling and psychotherapy sessions. Over a period of time and during several sessions, their problem was analysed systematically.

Even their daughter was given multiple counselling sessions. The sessions and therapy combined, helped calm her mind and channelize her thoughts. She was finally stable at mind and deed. At present, the family is well and happy together. The child wins a lot of prizes in her school competitions.

THOUGHTS:

Reluctance is the reason we don't take our plans to action. Hesitation to implement our plans results in procrastination. But, it is a fact that reluctance and hesitation are interlinked. We often tend to underestimate our own lives owing to these two factors. We get insecure and lose faith in ourselves while worrying about what others will think about us. This manifests as a mental stiffening. In such a case, even though your intellect differentiates between right and wrong, your reluctance and hesitation become your prime barriers. There is a lot of difference between knowing something and doing the same thing. For example, everyone knows that gratitude and forgiveness are both great virtues. But, do we practice them in our daily lives?

GRATITUDE:

The attitude of expressing our gratitude, reaps us rich rewards. To begin with, we need to get used to being grateful for what we have. Being grateful to God simply for existing and living is where we need to start with. Seek fulfilment in things you see around you. Growing up without knowing gratitude can be menacing for the society. Such children will not be thankful for the resources they are experiencing daily and this can cause many complications in the society. Parents should set an example to their children by expressing their gratitude frequently, from the milkman they meet every morning and to everyone else whose services they have taken, till bedtime.

It is easy to be grateful when you are in a comfortable and happy state of mind. But even when we experience difficult situations, we should be thankful for the experience we've got through it. Being thankful for what we have gives us the opportunity to express gratitude for many more things in life.

FORGIVENESS:

"It is human nature to do mistakes and it is divine nature to forgive" ---- A Pope.

It is sensible if you realise the mistakes made by you and apologise for the problems caused by them. In today's civilised society, apologies are made only for the sake of sustaining relationships. Refusing to forgive churns up different kinds of ideas and accumulates thoughts of being hurt and being deceived in the mind. When such thoughts constantly occur in mind, it leads to physical and mental illness. When you hate yourself, you are bound to hate others too. This is the fundamental thing. People who do not know how to love self, hate others. Life becomes beautiful when we accustom ourselves to accepting our own flaws. The world can then be seen in a completely different perspective.

The most important virtue which everyone should have is forgiveness. By forgiving wholeheartedly, we experience a positive feeling within ourselves. Psychologists say that forgiveness can prevent depression and curb that desire for revenge. Forgiving others with compassion can help love grow within us. A thankful person can forgive others easily.

EXERCISES:

WAYS TO APPRECIATE AND FORGIVE:

1. When you start appreciating others for small things, the jealousy within us will begin to fade gradually.
2. When you take care of the good things of others and compliment them, people will be drawn towards you. When you appreciate the good things in people, you gain their attention. You will develop a relation with

them and your friendship with them develops. They will recognise you as a person who knows the value of things and can perform good tasks. You will be considered respectable by people.

3. Love is a by-product of appreciation. These emotions give a sense of security. This is what gains trust, respect and value to a relationship.

4. Your environment and surroundings will change when you start appreciating and being thankful. People who associate with you will love you, be it in family, at office or in the community.

5. Appreciate everyone with an open mind. People actually yearn appreciation. You would be expanding the self-confidence of the person whom you are appreciating.

6. Forgiveness has the power to restore a relationship and add beauty to it. Only the person who knows how to respect others, will master the art of apologising appropriately.

7. List the unforgivable events and people on your mind. Write down 'I sincerely forgive all of you.', 21times a day for 30 consecutive days. Your mind will be ready to forgive.

8. If you carry feelings of pain, frustration, shame, anger, and sadness caused by others in your life, you might soon face psychosomatic illness. However, if you develop a lofty thought of forgiving and forgetting those events, you will be able to live with good physical and mental health.

9. You cannot change the past events and negative feelings which emerge from those memories. If your approach and attitude changes, u will be able to relieve yourself.

10. Life will be easier if we learn to ask and give forgiveness.

CHAPTER EIGHT

NEED AND DESIRE

He who is accustomed to subdue himself will not be attracted to anything else. Only he who has such merit deserves to live well in the world. -- Swami Vivekananda.

In today's consumerism based culture, men and women are tempted by various things the world has to offer. Because of this reason, they are facing several problems. Each of them have their own set of cravings and inclinations. It is not wrong to desire something. But being overzealous or obstinately obsessed about a thing is wrong. For every human being, fulfilment of needs leads to various desires being born. To fulfil our desires, we often choose to forage onto different paths. As quoted in a certain movie's song, "The more you explore, the lovelier your life will be. " In the same way, if every person keeps exploring onto new paths, he can progress to whatever position he aspired for.

EVENTS:

A middle class family were living in an apartment. The family consisted of father, mother and son. The other students in the apartment were studying in an international school. The parents observed the other children and felt that if their son had studied in that school, he too would speak fluent English. They would then be very proud of their son and would be respected in their society. So, they admitted him into the international school through a recommendation letter. However, the school fees was exorbitantly beyond their means.

Initially, when they saw their son speaking English fluently as they expected, they were happy and felt that their effort was worthwhile. So, even though they were facing a lot of financial pressure, they did not reveal their difficult situation to their son. He was in 6th standard. At school, he used to copy whatever his fellow students did. Then, he would come home and express some of his desires to his parents. The parents would fulfil his wishes for his happiness. One day, he came home and said that his friends and their parents were going to a foreign location for their summer holidays. He expressed his desire to go on a foreign tour with his parents, just like his peers. His wish astonished the parents. They finally revealed their financial situation to him. But he did not pay heed to any of their words. He would pertinaciously ask the same thing every day, but the parents did not respond to his obstinacy. Not able to bear his stubbornness, they decided to change his school. To this, the boy threatened his parents with his life. He angrily said that he didn't want to be alive if they did not comply to his wishes. Not knowing what to do, the parents came to see me with their son.

QUESTIONS TO PONDER OVER FROM THE ABOVE EVENTS:

1. Did the parents teach their son the difference between necessity and desire?
2. Is the boy's reaction the result of peer-influence or peer pressure?

DESCRIPTION:

The parents today do not teach their children the difference between necessity and desire. Today's parents themselves are attracted towards the current consumerism based culture. Desires overwhelm the minds of people. But differentiating the feeling of desire from necessity, according to our financial situation is an art. Most people experience anger when their expectations are not met. But if his wishes and desires are fulfilled whatsoever, greed enters in. Whoever understands the difference between desires and necessity, he starts exploring wisely and forages into new pathways.

The boy while seeing his peers at school, got influenced by their exorbitant lifestyle. Each family has expenditure based on their financial situation. Letting our children know about these household issues isn't wrong. On the other hand, if these things are unknown to them, they might react stubbornly or angrily when their wishes aren't fulfilled. Lot of parents do not understand weather their child is facing peer pressure or is under peer influence. When a child is influenced by his/her peers, peer pressure is validated. Influence from peers is observing the behaviour and ways of his friends and reflecting on it. The boy, in this case did the same thing. Peer pressure means being influenced by his friends and they in turn forcing him or bullying him to do the same thing together. This situation is quite evident during the teenage because they tend to believe and listen to their peers ideas and expressions.

Parents were given counselling on how to give freedom with responsibility to their children. They were made aware of the various consumerism based traps in our society and how this particular culture is dominating people and creating problems for us.

The boy was counselled over several sessions. He was enlightened about the meaning of freedom and duty. He was taught how to handle anger, how to accept various life events, and other problems he faced.

He was admitted into another school, where he has been concentrating on his academics and extracurricular activities. He is now a district level champion in Table Tennis.

THOUGHTS:

Instead of buying children whatever they desire, buy whatever is their necessity. Most of the times, parents buy fancy products for their children reminiscing that they could not own those fancy things in their childhood. In such cases, the children would not differentiate between necessity and desire. If you buy something which is not an absolute requirement, it won't have any value to it. Children should be taught responsibility from home. Try to give them small responsibilities at home, according to their age and capability. Only if they get used to things like this, they will be able to build leadership quality in themselves.

Nowadays, the parents are pampering their children excessively. Because of this, the qualities like problem handling abilities, valuing and understanding others and respecting others are becoming oblivious in children. Pampering children · increases their expectations from parents. Unnecessary expectations leads to disappointment, which in turn, leads to sadness and depression.

Each child and adult has different needs and desires. We can know it in 2 stages. 1ˢᵗ stage is analysing the situation, the experience and the education. 2ⁿᵈ stage is determining the place and person. All the five, determine whether it is necessity or desire. The flame of desire in each person makes him explore and forage into new worlds. Encouraging them causes their success to flow beyond their expectations. At home and school, during their first 2 years of age, their talent and interests develop. If moulded on the same path, they are likely to succeed in their lives.

EVENTS:

HOW TO TEACH CHILDREN TO IDENTIFY THEIR NECESSITIES:

1. Desires bud from fulfilment of necessities. But, that is the exact desire which needs to be curbed.

2. Abolishing desires is not an easy task. Rather, it would be wise to realign your desires and live prosperously.

3. The true nature of the mind is that of a wanderer. Subduing our mind with good thoughts is a wise way to go.

4. If we do not explore enough, we would face lack of opportunities.

5. If necessity and exploration is the foundation of discoveries, then passion and the flame for fulfilment is the foundation of necessity and exploration. Often, our experiences help us to become free from chaotic situations.

6. Thoughts arise within us both as need and desire, depending on what is essential for us. This is natural. We can live our life to the fullest if our will to fulfil our necessity is stauncher than that of our desires.

7. When unnecessary desires take birth in mind, we make efforts to achieve it. This can cause suffering and depression.

8. It is vital that our desires comply to our financial situation so that it does not disturb our peace of mind.

9. When you make unnecessary purchases, you may not be able to avail things when you face necessities. So avoid unnecessary expenditure.

10. The ultimate necessity of anyone is content and happiness. Just question yourself and let your conscience answer!

CHAPTER NINE

REALIGNING OUR MIND IN DIFFICULT TIMES

Not all problems are stressful. Some problems can also act as a trigger for us to develop and exhibit our talents. -- Copmeyer.

Everyone will have experienced joy, sorrow, success and failure in their life. There is no one on this planet who has experienced just success throughout life. Similarly, there is none who has experienced just failure throughout life. Success and failure are the two sides of the same coin. Success depends on the attitude of the individual. Failure can either make or break an individual. Depending on how we deal with it, failure teaches us many experimental lessons in our life. It helps you recognise your priorities. It makes you understand what is important in your life. Failure teaches us to feel others' pain and to be kind.

EVENTS:

There lived a family of three. The mother and the father were into business. They had a son. He had scored over 1000 marks in his 12th class. The elated parents agreed on his wish to study in a college in Bangalore. However, due to late admission, he couldn't find a place in the hostel. So he had to take a room outside the campus.

He started to share a room with some of the fellow students in a mansion and started attending college from there. There were no big restrictions in the mansion where he was living. So they started to go for frequent outings, movies and hotels. Thus, he started bunking college. He even had a girlfriend in the college. The friendship transformed into love in no time and, soon, he even had a breakup. As a result, his routine life changed and had several addictions. He could not concentrate on his studies. So he got an arrear in his first semester. When his parents questioned him about it, he gave an excuse that he was in a new environment, it was his 1st year there, and so he was facing some problems coping up. He also complained of insufficient pocket money. His parents, thus convinced, increased his allowance. Then, he started spending a lot. Even in his second year of college, he got arrears. This time, his parents condemned him strictly and demanded an explanation. This time, he convinced them saying that his syllabus was difficult and that he would write all of it together and pass. But then, he stopped attending his classes and his examinations. Then his professors too started questioning his behaviour.

Facing constant failures, he lost his self-confidence. His way of life and his nature changed. He started drinking and smoking daily. He wouldn't even call his parents. So, one day, his parents visited him as a surprise. When they did not find him at the mansion, they thought that he went out somewhere, so they waited patiently for him near the mansion. After some time, his roommate arrived. So they entered the room with him. They noticed the presence of empty alcohol bottles and cigarette butts around. Seeing that, they were disgusted and fumed with anger. Later they saw their son drunk and swinging around. The angry parents at once compelled him to come home with them. Following this, they came to see me with their son.

QUESTIONS TO PONDER UPON ROM THE ABOVE EVENTS:

1. Why did he drown himself in failure and couldn't revert back to his good old ways normally?

2. Why couldn't he accept his failure as a stepping stone for success?

3. Why did the student forget the reason he chose that particular college?

DESCRIPTION:

There are no one in life who have not experienced failures. Small or big, some sort of failure stays with us all our life. For many people, small failures do not affect much. But, when people face failure in their occupation or life goals or with things which are very dear to them in life, they are heartbroken. Failure teaches us many lessons as we grow, mature and live life. It helps us recognise the true nature of people surrounding us. When failures wound us and we successfully relieve ourselves from that wound, we get to experience new relationships, learn new lessons and achieve tremendous success.

The reason for the student's failure in the event was his inability to recover, lack of self-control, bad companionship, forgetting his purpose of joining the college, his consequent actions after forgetting his ambitions and his bitter experiences transforming into failures. The reason him not being able to accept his failure as a lesson was because his mind was deeply hurt and he took those failures emotionally. He started worrying about what others might think about him. He knew that his parents had complete faith in him. Hence, out of guilt, he could not even face them. Inferiority complex gripped his mind. He completely forgot his ambition and failed to utilise his freedom in a correct way. At a time when he should be focussed on making a career, he fell in love and engaged in bad habits and lacked self-control. All these factors together made him forget his purpose of coming to that college.

Parents were counselled separately on how to change their habits and attitude to support their son and help him overcome the situation. Simultaneously, the student too received counselling sessions in which the psychologist tried to realign his mind and helped him prioritise his options in life. After several sessions, he got better. Presently, he is in a college in Chennai, pursuing his Masters Degree.

THOUGHTS:

Life is like a bus journey. There are a lot of stops during the journey. If there is an obstacle, you have to change your route. Sometimes you might even face accidents. You meet new people on your journey, face new events and situations. In the same way, failure and success comes alternatively in everyone's life. But, in this generation, no one understands that. Because, each one us look forward only to tasting success. People are unable to take the bitterness of failure and the experience lesson which comes along with it. Failures strengthen us from within. In today's generation, unable to face failures, most people opt committing suicide. The downside is, in our country, the suicide rate is increasing every day.

Everyone faces non-fulfilment in their life, in different ways. For example, students failing in exam, failing in sports competitions, youth failing in love and adults failing in married life or in business. Losing something or someone very dear causes heartbreak. All these are accounted for as failures. But, there are lot of people in the world who have raced against these problems and won over them. That was because they never let their self-confidence recede at any point of time. Success can never be achieved in one day. Only through failures, your skill and talent can be realized and utilized completely. We can recognise our true friends only during our failure. If we take our failures as an event in our journey of life rather than as an emotion, the same failures will become a stepping stone for our success.

EXERCISE:
METHODS TO FACE FAILURES:

1. Repeat the words of hope, "it will change" in your mind. Believe that no matter what situation you are in right now, this will change.

2. Most people continue doing things in the same way over years. But, with time, new developments happen and old methods get outdated. Most people fail to realise this. Try to create a mentality of trying new things or trying a different way to do things.

3. Do not dwell in your past. It has passed some time ago. You can neither change it nor plan anything about it. Learn to live in the present and plan for your future.

4. Each of us have certain inborn qualities and thoughts within us. They are present in us since our birth. We get them hereditarily, with situations, by our thoughts and according to our nature. However ingrained they might be, you need to adapt yourself with the change of time and circumstances to newer ways of life and technology.

5. Mr. Iraianbu I.A.S , once said," Every failure is an experience. Each failure teaches us a lot of lessons which assist in our growth and help us mature. It also helps us recognise and understand others and ultimately, in realizing life.

6. If you take failures emotionally, it can hurt you. You should realize that failure is not the end of the road for you. There will still be plenty of opportunities ahead

of you. You should learn to face life with the hope and confidence of finding them.

7. A failure will either destroy you or will carve out the best version of you. That will depend on how you decide to deal with that incident and navigate through your present.

8. Practice saying "I lost" rather than saying "I did not succeed". This will encourage you to try repeatedly and will keep the flame burning within you.

9. Do not expect every day to be a day of harvest. On the contrary, every day of yours could be a day for sowing.

10. "The bolder you act, the more rewarding your life will be." ---- Robin Sharma. Dare to live your life to the fullest.

PART - 3 (RELATIONSHIPS)

NO MATTER WHAT THE RELATIONSHIP IS, IF YOU ACCEPT THEM AS A PART OF YOURSELF, THEY WILL ALWAYS SHARE A MAGNIFICIENT RELATIONSHIP WITH YOU. --- SADHGURU

CHAPTER TEN

DIFFERENCES BETWEEN HOME AND HOSTEL

WHATEVER WE NEED TO DO, IF WE DO CORRECTLY, THEN WHATEVER HAS TO COME TO US, WILL MAKE ITS WAY TO US. - SWAMI VIVEKANANDA

Previously, people used to consider their home to be their temple. But today, homes are becoming like hostels. People nowadays, do not bear the capacity to think straight and be righteous. Most people are living their life off without understanding the importance and value of relationships. Home is a place where the family is bound together with emotions of love and care for each other. It is a place where happiness is shared. Some people search for happiness outside home.

Home is a place where people communicate with each other and strengthen their relationship over time. When homes were small, families were large. On the contrary, when homes became large, families became small. And so has the love and affection towards one other.

EVENTS:

There was a family consisting of father, mother and daughter. The daughter had completed her studies and was ready for marriage. Her parents had brought her up in a luxurious lifestyle. She was their only daughter. So they would fulfil every wish of hers, lovingly. Even if she did a mistake, her parents would adjust accordingly, taking care not to hurt her feelings. Soon, there came the appropriate time to search for a suitable groom for her. They found an idealistic groom soon. Then followed the engagement ceremony. Soon enough the wedding date was fixed and she was married off at the destined date.

But soon, the rosy time came to an end and she started having lot of problems in her married life. She could not accommodate to the ways of her husband's family. So she constantly faced criticism and problems in her daily life.

For example, at her parents' home, she used to wake up at around 10 a.m. and her mother would bring her coffee. But, in her husband's home, she had to wake up at 7 a.m. So, she found it really difficult to adapt to her new life there. As she always woke up late, she found it difficult to wake up early. She used to have complete freedom at her parents' home. But she did not utilise it properly. She could not even bring herself to do small chores for self. Since she was habituated that way since her childhood and did not know otherwise, she imagined the whole world to be the same. She had imagined even her in-laws place to be the same. So, the couple faced problems daily. She could not bear those problems and slipped into depression and negative thoughts. So, her husband had brought her to me for counselling.

QUESTIONS TO PONDER UPON FROM THE ABOVE EVENTS:

1. Have the parents failed in their duty and responsibility to impart knowledge of duties and responsibilities to their daughter?
2. Did her luxurious lifestyle at her parents' home help in her growth in any way?
3. What is the cause of her depression and anxiety issues at her in-laws home?

DESCRIPTION:

The girl's parents had given her complete freedom, but she could not utilise it properly. The parents gave her an immensely carefree life, but did not teach her the responsibility and duties which come along with age. Because of that, she could not build any decision making ability and so, grew up as a dependant woman. She grew up sans all that knowledge at every stage of life. But, she couldn't escape them after marriage. She had been living in a fictional world all along before her marriage. However, when she had to face her duties and responsibilities post marriage, she was unable to come out of her fictional bubble of luxury. This paved way for more complications in her daily life. Her affluent lifestyle regressed her life into negativity, which resulted in despair and depression. She was unable to confide in anyone or discuss her issues with anyone. She mused over her troublesome situations over and over again which lead to her developing an inferiority complex. Gradually, due to low dignity of self, sleeplessness, intentional skipping of meals and depression, her thoughts, actions and behaviour altogether changed.

The couple attended several sessions of psychological counselling in which topics like family welfare and ideal attitude towards each other were discussed. The sessions were designed to invoke new progressive line of thought about how to handle her issues. The sessions also helped her stabilise her mind and inculcated the awareness about family life and societal norms. As a result of many sessions thus, she developed a personality about herself where she was aware of her duties and responsibilities and would willingly accomplish them all by herself. Thus, she lived contentedly with her husband and children.

THOUGHTS:

Our lives can be divided into three categories. Category one are the survivors. They struggle for their survival everyday monotonously without a strategy. Category two are the ones who are just 'existing'. These people live their life based on their small savings from time to time. Category three are the people who are 'living their life'. These people believe that everyday gives you new opportunities and that you need to put in sufficient efforts to grab them. They strive to uplift themselves towards triumph.

This current generation is classified mostly into category one or two. Very little percentage of people are included in category three. When you meet someone and enquire about their wellbeing, most would reply," Ah! Am surviving somehow". The source of such an answer might be their feeling of deficit of the warmth of a home. At hostels, there are authorities who need you to follow some rules and guidelines. They, sort of tend to control your actions. However, home is a place where you are free to act your way but you get to practice self-control. The third category of people actually possess this quality. When others control your way of life, it would be called as 'existing". Many people fail to recall their duties towards their home. If we carry out our responsibilities and duties willingly and whole heartedly, we would not despise them. However, if the same is being done without any interest or willingness, then it seems an uphill task. Winners are those who carry out their tasks by consciously involving self into them.

To become parents, we ought to come down to the level of children first. There is no proper dictated or noted procedure for raising children or for child care. Every child's nature and approach will naturally be different. Circumstances play an important role in raising a child. There are two parts in that. In the first part, the family members' participation influences the growth and development of a child in multiple ways. In the second part, neighbours, school, and the society which we live in extends assistance or helps towards child growth. It is an essential requisite that children be supported by parents, psychologically, in any given situation.

EXERCISES:

WAYS TO DEVELOP GOOD RELATIONSHIPS AT HOME:

1. Understanding relationships, tolerance and a spirit of sharing are essential for maintaining a relationship. This stabilises a relationship and helps living together in unity.
2. It is alright to be in a relationship, based on a motive. Not being able to communicate, can cause parting of ways for no apparent reason at all.
3. The foundation for all relationships is Trust. We generally start doubting when our hope starts to diminish. This might cause estrangement. So, it is important not to lose hope in order for the relationship to last long.

4. Relationships bonded by love are timeless. During an argument, whoever is ready to give up the bickering and ask forgiveness is the one who cares more about the relationship rather than the argument.

5. Do not be bound by your ego. You should bear the attitude of giving up an argument to prevent the problem from exaggerating.

6. Examine your capabilities with an open mind. It would be easier if you could distinguish between small and unimportant things and larger issues. This is vital when it comes to repairing relationships.

7. When you communicate with children with physical contact, they tend to understand better. It increases their love and trust for you.

8. Feelings wax and wane from time to time. When emotionally present, try to resolve your problems. Maintaining relationships is an art.

9. Whatever the relation might be, sharing of love and affection is a must. Be ever ready to impart love and affection, wholeheartedly. Do whatever it takes to fulfil the expectations of your loved ones. If you can do that, you will be recognised as a reliable person whom people can turn to in times of need.

10. It is necessary to have a pleasantness in our relationships. We need to build relations which can stand by us and lend a shoulder to lean on, in our difficult times. Try to be the change you need in others.

CHAPTER ELEVEN

ARE YOU ALONE OR LONELY

THOSE WHO ENTHUSIASTICALLY PUT IN EFFORTS TO OVERCOME THEIR FAILURES, BECOME SUCCESSFUL HUMAN BEINGS. -- WINSTON CHURCHILL

Human beings depend on each other for various necessities from their birth till their death. Humans are social animals, who enjoy cohabiting. Some people, however, prefer living independently. Most people in this world are forced to live alone due to circumstances. There is a thin line of difference between living alone and being lonely.

Loneliness is the state of suffering from being isolated intentionally by others. The uniqueness is, some people present themselves and their tasks elegantly and differently by being isolated. Individuality shouldn't change to loneliness. However, people in both the stages, who try their best to maintain their individuality, grow well.

EVENTS:

There lived a family of four consisting of father, mother and their two children. Both the parents were government employees. The daughter was in the 1st year of college. The son was in 7th class. The girl was a talented personality and a bright student. But, mostly, she preferred to be alone. She would not socialise much. If someone spoke to her, she would hesitate to reply or silently avoid them. She would be a fun-loving individual when around her friends at college and with her brother. But, for some reason, she would lament that she was not able to celebrate her happiness. She would grumble at her parents that they were neglecting her. Her parents did not mind her words much because she was scoring quite well in her examinations. So they did not even mind her preferring to be alone most of the time. Since she was the same way even in her college, her friends too, didn't mind much because they felt that she preferred it that way.

Once, their professor asked the class to divide themselves into groups of five for a project. Instantly, the entire class grouped themselves accordingly. When she went to join in a group, they rejected her and did not allow her to join. The children in other groups too cited some or the other reasons to avoid her. Usually, when she would herself stay aloof, she wouldn't feel dejected. But, when her friends rejected her, she felt extremely hurt and started to hate them all. This rejection formed strong memories in her mind and she would get disturbed by the thoughts again and again. Gradually, she slipped into depression. These feelings mixed with her daily life caused differences in her thought process and behaviour. One day, at the dinner table with her parents, she announced that she wasn't interested to live anymore. Saying thus, she locked herself in her room. The parents, shocked, tried their might at breaking the door open. Finally, when they succeeded and entered the room, they found her attempting suicide by cutting her wrist with a knife. They immediately pulled her away and saved her. She was taken to a hospital and was given first aid immediately. Then, the girl, accompanied by the parents, came to meet me.

QUESTIONS TO PONDER FROM THE ABOVBE EVENTS:

1. Did the parents realise the difference between being alone and feeling lonely?
2. Why did the girl prefer being alone most of the time?
3. Is her suicide attempt a correct way to find solution to her issues?

DESCRIPTION

Nowadays, when some children stay aloof, their parents assume that it is their individuality. Many parents today see uniqueness in whatever their children do or however they behave. They do not realize that really unique children will tend to approach the common situations in a different way. Loneliness is an emotional tragedy which struck them in their life. Feelings like distress, sorrow, disappointment and some unfinished incidents of the past keep haunting their mind. These emotions complicate their personality and they do not know how to come out of it. Hence, they tend to prefer being alone. The parents in the above event, did not understand the difference between loneliness and being alone. Well, to find out the cause of the student's loneliness, we need to look into her life during her teenage years. She was looked down upon by her class mates and teased because of her looks. She was made fun of, by saying that she had a masculine body and voice. This criticism impacted her a lot. She struggled a lot to get over her feelings and finally, switched schools after her 10th grade.

But, switching schools could not decrease her inferiority complex. Even in the new school, she could not communicate freely with her co-students. She used to carry her books even to the playground. She would not play with anyone. This kind of behaviour of hers seemed awkward and different to the other students.

Every child's problem has a root somewhere in the past. If it is explored and approached in the right way, there is a chance to overcome it. There is nothing wrong in asking for help when you cannot handle some of your problems by yourself. The youth in today's generation, however, feel it is inferior of themselves to seek help. Thus they are often hesitant and do not dare to ask for assistance. Only the courageous seek help.

The student in the above event described, weaponised suicide. That was never a right solution. People in distress often search permanent solutions for temporary problems. For some different reason, suicide is nowadays the only solution for every problem. According to statistics, the young generation are often opting suicide. Tamil Nadu ranks first in this. When we are in distress, the problem in which we are in, seems like a narrow steep ridge. Our thought process will be narrow minded when we are in problems. If we review the same situation after a period of one week or one month, when our mind calms down, it will seem to be an entirely different situation. The current generation is not willing to counter the challenges of life. The parents should allow children to face their own problems and handle their own situations from a young age.

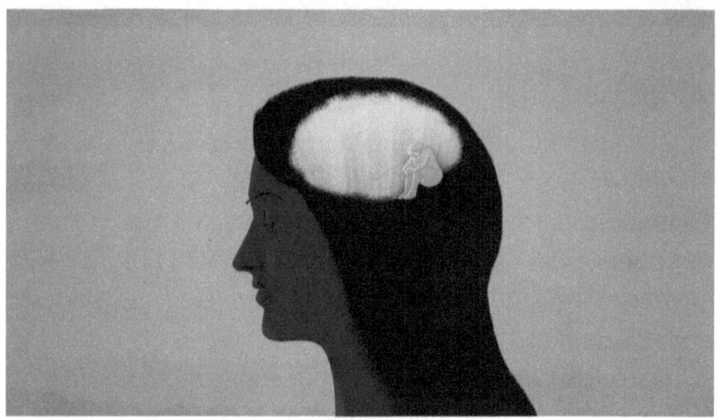

Over some sessions, the parents explained the importance of spending time with their children. The girl was offered counselling sessions for negative thoughts recurring in her mind. The inferiority complex which had become ingrained in her personality and her hormonal imbalance was tried to be reversed. She was counselled in detail on topics like how to handle bullying and negative comments by peers. She was explained comprehensively about handling that kind of circumstances. After multiple sessions, there was a considerable improvement in her speech, line of thought, behaviour and personality. Currently, she is pursuing post-graduation.

THOUGHTS:

People who do not understand themselves completely, prefer living in solitude. In our modern life, loneliness is affecting many individuals and pushing them into the brink of depression. Physical and behavioural changes are evident in depressed people. Loneliness may affect just one person, but his behavioural changes effects the entire community around him. The characteristic of living with others as a community is constant in human life. With the development of civilization and the changes that have taken place along with it, there is more competition around than before. We should constantly update our knowledge, try to learn new things and strive to implement the same. If we do not, then depending on others for our necessities becomes imminent.

The children of today's generation somehow depend on others habitually, even for insignificant needs. This attitude becomes an obstacle for growth. While some parents raise their children to be dependent on them, some children prefer to be dependent on their parents. This may be attributed to them being lazy and not wanting to work and to escape from their duties.

People who possess uniqueness in their thought and attitude, create a new path for themselves and strive to go along the same path. Their skill and talent speaks for them. They will have the capacity to face any situation differently and craft any situation to their benefit. This quality alone will push them towards success in business, education, jobs and relationships. These people go ahead as guides for others. This kind of people succeed by adapting to the problems and challenges they face to their own advantage.

EXERCISES:

HOW TO RAISE CHILDREN WITH INDIVIDUALITY:

1. Reluctance and fear are obstacles for development. If you identify the same and try to come out of your emotional state, it makes you a unique person with individuality.
2. If you want to act differently, you have to think differently. That's the way to become successful in businesses, workplace, relationships and even life.
3. Success does not kiss everyone all the time. It takes some extraordinary efforts for that. We should get to know self, better. Then, try to understand others' situations and work differently. Only then, can we see the horizons of success.
4. Sometimes, you might come across people who mock your uniqueness. Instead of taking it to heart, you must realize that the uniqueness is your identity. Creating a new path and travelling on it is not an easy task.
5. Find the best way to recover from the crisis. You must remember that difficult times are faced by everyone. Rise with all your might when you fall. Always keep moving forward. Only then, the path itself will start forming for you.
6. You must consciously allow only positive thoughts to form in your mind. By doing so, your body and mind will be energised throughout the day. You will be able to navigate through your day with a smile.
7. Try to be a guide for others. If you come across anyone facing similar issues like yours, try to help them out by sharing your take on the problem. Do not hesitate to

share the solution you had applied to overcome a similar situation. If you practice this, you can recover from the worst kind of failure. Your unique approach to solving issues will make you a leader.

8. While everyone is taking care of today's issues, you ought to think of tomorrow's problems. Uniqueness is about a way to prevent a problem from cropping up rather than looking for a solution.

9. Do not expect to win in all discussions or arguments. You must think about an existing alternative or try to create an alternative.

10. Try to have a conversation with self in your mind. You will be surprised to know your own strengths and weakness. The depth of your thoughts can reveal a lot of new things. Choose to follow its voice.

CHAPTER TWELVE

TELECOMMUNICATION CREATING A DISTANCE IN RELATIONSHIPS

HUMAN RELATIONSHIPS ARE BOUND BY LOVE. ONLY WHEN WE TRAVEL ACROSS THE BRIDGE OF LOVE, WILL OUR LIVES BE MEANINGFUL AND COMFORTABLE. ---- TAGORE.

Television is occupyinga definite place in every home nowadays. In olden days, it used to be a luxury. But, in recent times, it has become a necessity. Off late, it is even becoming an interference in relationships at homes. Televisions and screens are attracting people of all ages. Children and adults are equally getting addicted to television and screens, thereby losing their mental restraints. According to some research articles, both the children and adults are losing their level-headedness while watching television.

EVENTS:

There lived a family of three. Both the parents were busy at work most of their time. The father was into business and the mother was managing a supermarket. They had a daughter who was studying in 4th class. The parents have arranged for a car for taking her to school and bringing her back. At home, they appointed a nanny and a cook to take care of her. The child would get whatever she needed on time, punctually. But, when she comes home from school, she didn't have anyone to talk to or play with. She would watch cartoon network on television till around 10p.m. Then having her dinner, she would sleep off. Most of the times, the parents would come home really late, often after she slept. Sometimes she would do her homework watching T.V and then would have dinner and sleep off. This was her daily routine.

One day, the teacher asked the students to write an essay about their friends as homework and read it aloud in class. The next day, each of the student read their essays out loud. Each of them had written about their real life friends and relationships and emotions. But, this particular girl wrote that her friends were Dora, teddy bear and television. She was the only girl who took cartoon network characters and toys to be her friends. This incident put the teacher in deep thought. She called the girl individually and had a little conversation with her. She understood the situation of the girl at home. The teacher felt sorry for her and took extra care of her. She would send her to the playground to play whenever she had time.

She called her parents and updated them about their daughter's academics and activities at school. She informed the parents about the girl's essay and her behaviour at the playground. She let them know that the child was speaking to herself most of the time and preferred not to play with her peers. She could not concentrate during her classes and would be in an imaginary world most of the time. The teacher opined that she needed more involvement from her parents. Hearing all this, the parents felt sorry about their daughter's emotional state of talking to self. Not knowing what to do, they came to see me along with their daughter.

QUESTIONS TO PONDER UPON FROM THE ABOVE EVENTS:

1. What is the reason behind the girl not having any friends?

2. What is the reason behind the emotional state of the child, talking to self?

DISCUSSION:

The child described in the above doesn't have any real friends. Only when children play outdoors with peers, they share thoughts and ideas and gain each other's friendship. This kind of opportunity can be seen mostly in schools. But this girl would stand apart lonely even at school. The circumstances around her and her experience through them had ingrained deep into her mind. Since she felt lonely without parental affection and caressing, she assumed the cartoon characters and her toys to be her friends. Since her parents did not allow her to play outdoors, without a human contact, her mind got confused over what proper human relations are.

Social bonding teaches a lot of things to children. However, it is necessary for the parents to be supportive. Exposure to various kinds of people and friends in our society from a very young age, supports mental development in children. The parents of the child are purely responsible for the current emotional state of the child, because they spent very little to almost no time with her. The child yearned the parents' affection and when she could not receive that, she got many thoughts in mind. She lived in an imaginary world of cartoons and toys or whatever she saw on the television. She imagined the same and would converse with them instead of real people.

The parents must spend sufficient time with their kids, get to know about their thoughts and their most innate voices. Their problem would be solved instantly. There is a short film in Tamil called Ekam. It is a must-see for every parent. This film portrays how a child yearns for her parent's affection in a very beautiful and sensitive way.

Initially, when she was brought to me, she was talking to herself. By the psychiatrist's opinion, in some sessions, the child was made to feel her parents' love and affection. They spent some time with her together and got to know more about her feelings. Through Art therapy, Play therapy and some cooperation from her parents, the child's mental state was stabilized. After some sessions, there was a small change observed in her behaviour. She was made to express her feelings and thoughts by encouraging her to converse via stories. This attempt strengthened her mental state. Currently, they are happily together.

To make sure this kind of circumstance doesn't repeat, parents should be able to cater sufficient time and shower their affection on their children. The presence of parents around the child itself provides great mental support to them. Currently, the child is in 6th class. She is participating in various group dances with her classmates and is winning various prizes.

THOUGHTS:

In today's modern culture, children are getting addicted to television and this is becoming a nuisance to the parents. In the past, the children in a family were close with their relatives. Today, the children desire to be close to devices and objects. Today's children do not know the importance of relationships with other people. Their declining interactions with other people is the reason they find it difficult to coexist with the community.

Excessive viewing of television causes loss of vision in children. So using spectacles from at an early age is becoming a necessity. When the children watch soft violence on cartoons, they try to imbibe the same and display an equally violent attitude with friends and peers.

On the whole, they are getting addicted to the cartoons and various other visuals on T.V. Insufficient exercise due to lack of outdoor activity has resulted in juvenile obesity. Due to watching T.V for ample hours, they are losing the ability to concentrate and are easily getting distracted. When in school, they are not able to focus in their classes. The bond between the parents and children is strengthened only by trust. When children do a mistake, parents should bear sufficient patience to be able to explain them effectively, about why their doing was wrong and about how not to repeat it.

EXERCISES:

HOW TO STRENGTHEN THE RELATION BETWEEN PARENTS AND CHILDREN:

1. Parents need to talk to children. Children yearn to be listened to and to express themselves to their parents. But if they do get to express themselves, they feel distant from parental affection. They get involved into television and cartoons so much so, that the T.V becomes their world. Not having any relation with the real outside world, they find it awkward and difficult accommodating to situations and people. To avoid this, parents must spend a lot of time with their children.

2. Television must be viewed as a source of entertainment. Care must be taken that television doesn't become a means to pass away time for children. If it becomes so, they tend to lose their self-control.

3. Children should play outdoors with their friends and mates. Only then, can they develop social skills. Outdoor games which involve children playing as a group, teach them qualities like leadership and team work.

4. Maintaining relationships is an art. Strengthening relations by initiating direct conversations is a skill.
5. Use your relationships with family, friends and colleagues to push yourself on the path to development.
6. Maintaining relationships is a journey. You can either make the journey a happy and joyful one or a sad and depressing one. It all depends on your perspective and attitude.
7. If you want the children in your family to grow in a disciplined way, the enthusiasm of the close knit family members will be helpful.
8. Make it a point to talk and communicate with all your family members before you retire for the day. This habit can keep relationships from falling apart.
9. If you use your relationships properly and streamline them appropriately, your talents will shine out. The world will be a better place to live in.
10. Our feelings and personality depends upon what we think most of the time. If you constantly think of your happy moments and the fulfilling things in your life, happiness will be guaranteed 100%.

CHAPTER THIRTEEN

COMMANDING AND CONCERNING

KIDS WOULD LOVE BEING NEAR AND AROUND YOU MORE THAN THE GIFTS YOU BUY FOR THEM. ---- JESSIE JACKSON

Despite the huge development of civilization around us, the relationship of mother and child, remains intact to this day. Hugging is not a new concept. It all just starts naturally when a baby is born. Hugging and caressing makes the child joyful and increases his/her faith. Thus, a bond of trust, love and confidence buds in the child's mind towards the parents. Children must be encouraged to face new endeavours and challenges independently.

EVENTS:

There lived a family of three. The father was a policeman. The mother was working in railway department. Their daughter was in 5th standard at a school. Both the parents would reach home after work at different timings. The grandparents of the girl lived nearby. So, whenever the parents were late from work, she would stay at her grandpa's place. She would play and do her homework there, while waiting for her parents. Sometimes, she would sleep off by the time they came home. In case they arrive early, she would talk and play with them for a bit and then would go to sleep. During the holidays, she would play jubilantly with her parents. They would spend the day cuddling her lovingly. The family were used to sleep together in the same room. One day, the girl complained of severe stomach pain. On rushing her to the hospital, they learnt that her menstrual cycle had initiated. The family celebrated the occasion. They held a function to perform some rituals accordingly.

After some days, the parents sat her down and said," Now that you have come of age, you should be having a room for yourself. You should get used to sleeping in your own room." This confused the girl.

Then, gradually with time, when her parents decreased their cuddling and caressing, she began to have different kind of thoughts. She suddenly started feeling that her parents did not like her anymore. She started to conceal her feelings and did not share her ideas or thoughts with anyone anymore.

After some days like this, she complained of severe headache, often. So the parents took her to see a doctor again. The doctor prescribed some medicines, but the meds did her no good. Her headache did not get any better. So the doctor decided to speak to the girl privately. Then, the doctor communicated with the parents and told them that their daughter had no physical problems at all. Rather, she was suffering psychologically. Hence, the headaches. So he suggested them to consult a psychologist for their daughter. Gathering this from the doctor, the parents came to see me with their daughter.

QUESTIONS TO PIONDER FROM THE ABOVE EVENTS:

1. What did the girl miss from parents that pushed her into such a psychological state?
2. What caused the girl to develop headache?

DESCRIPTION:

The root cause of the child's current state is that the child did not receive the required amount of love, affection, warmth, and caressing from the parents. The stress accumulate due the above stated reason resulted in headache. As soon as the daughter came of age, the parents provided her a different room to stay in. But, since they were quite close to her previously, this sudden change has led her to a state of confusion. She had illusions that her parents were avoiding her or did not like her anymore. Continuously pining for their affection and not being able to receive it from them caused stress in her, which surfaced in the form of headaches.

So, the girl was given several sessions of therapy via art and play. These sessions were designed to instil self-confidence and faith in her. The parents too, were counselled on how important it was to express their love in various ways to their children. They were emphasized on the fact that their loving touch and caressing would bridge the gap between the parents and the children and would enable greater understanding between them.

The changed attitude of the parents has started to show significant development in the girl. She started participating in several competitions and even won 1st prize in district level drawing competition.

THOUGHTS:

When kids are hugged and caressed, their bodies secrete the 'happy hormones' and keep their emotions balanced. They feel safe and deeply attached to the parents. It helps in developing and dealing with their emotions. While hugging children, through the wordless silence, parents can reach their emotions and develop an understanding with the children. Love can help transcend emotions and barriers. We can win over children with affection and love rather than harsh condemnation or ordering them around. When the children are angry or upset, they can be calmed down by giving them a tight hug and patting them and caressing them. This will bring about optimistic feelings and a disciplined attitude.

When parents treat their children respectfully and decently, their happy hormones start showing up. Condemning them and imposing orders on them will curb their emotions and clip their freedom. Some parents keep ordering their children around, imposing instructions as if clumping bricks during construction. This creates a distance between the parents and children. As a result, they tend to become close to their friends. As per psychology, a child needs to be hugged at least 8 times per day. Love is crucial for mental and physical development of a child.

Some couples yearn for children. In the same way, there are a lot of children who yearn for their parents' affection, endlessly. The young generation couples today are opting for separation or divorce rather than trying to discuss and solve their issues. Love and an attempt to understand each other is essential for such discussions to turn to reality.

EXERCISES:
HOW TO EXPRESS LOVE TO CHILDREN:

1. Love is something which cannot be seen, can only be expressed. The only way to express it to children, physically is by cuddling them. This is an essential way to convey our innate affection for them.
2. Only love has the power to change the world for the better. If parents express their love for their children without fussing, they will experience their children's fondness for them, multiple-fold.

3. When homes and relationships shrink in size, love between people too shrinks. Extra efforts should be made to increase the stability between relationships.
4. Set aside time every day to communicate with others in the family. Try to cultivate fondness and love for each other. Extend your experience to your social life too.
5. Make it a point to communicate with everyone in the family. This will help strengthen your understanding for each other.
6. Try to extend small help to your children in ways they won't expect. Surprise them often. This will make them feel recognised and important.
7. The fundamental feeling in all relationships is love. if you express your genuine concern and fondness for someone, (be it relative/friend/family), it will definitely return to you multi-fold.
8. Love between relations expands when an open mind is maintained. When you speak with respect and an open mind, people will automatically trust you.
9. Stay respectful and supportive to each other. Strive to decrease your expectations and get to know the ground reality of things. Tread accordingly.
10. It is necessary to attend events with your entire family. It provides an opportunity to introduce your relations to your children. In such cases, love transcends generations.

CHAPTER FOURTEEN

PATIENCE AND JEALOUSY

Traverse your obstacles and outperform yourself. When you wait with patience, your peace, happiness and remuneration will themselves approach you. ---- John Kein Auckfield

Inculcate the art of listening patiently when communicating with others. This calibre of yours will establish a beautiful relationship and faithfulness with people around you. Only love and affection in one's mind can bring about the virtue of patience in their personality. Just like clarity is important in conversations, so is patience to nurture and develop leadership. People with illusions that they do not have enough or they could not do enough, often breed feelings of jealousy and impatience.

EVENTS:

There lived a family of four, father, mother and their two children. The elder one was their son. He was in 4th standard at school. His younger sister was just 3 years old. The boy used to be quite good at studies and was an obedient child. But, since the time his sister was born, his attitude changed a lot. He began feeling competitive with his baby sister for their parents' affection. He would often beat her up and make her cry. The parents, though troubled, did not understand the dire necessity for correcting this particular attitude of his. They did not take any steps to curb his behaviour.

One day, the father was at a nearby shop and the mother was in the kitchen, cooking. The boy picked up his baby sister and wearing his slippers, went to the terrace in that scorching heat of the sun. He made her stand there with just bare feet. She was distressed and was in pain. So, she started wailing. Hearing the cry, the father who was nearby, rushed to the terrace and was shocked to see the boy forcing her to stand upright in the hot sun. He instantly hit his son and picking his daughter up, went downstairs. He related the entire event to his wife. The parents sat their son down and reprimanded him for his act. They strictly asked him not to repeat such activities.

Days passed. One day, he took her to the terrace again and pushed her down the stairs. The little baby started bleeding profusely and was wailing out of pain. The mother rushed to the spot and the boy informed her that his sister had fallen down all by herself. She was terrified to see the little girl's head bleeding profusely and rushed her to the hospital. She was given timely first aid and was thus saved. Later, the parents related the entire sequence of events between the siblings, to the doctor. On hearing everything in a detailed manner, the doctor suggested the necessity of a psychologist for the boy. He said that if the psychologist understood the boy's mind-set and treated him correctly, his complicated thoughts could be resolved. Then the parents along with the boy, came to meet me.

QUESTIONS TO PONDER FROM THE ABOVE EVENTS:

1. What is the reason the boy could not accept his sister?
2. Was the affection of the parents seem insufficient to him after the birth of his sister?

DESCRIPTION:

The reason the boy could not accept his sister and saw her as a competition for his parents' affection is his lack of knowledge about siblings and how older siblings treat younger ones. This knowledge should have been imparted by the parents to him since the time she was pregnant for the second time. The parents needed to prepare their son mentally by explaining him about the foetus and the about-to-come baby. In such a case, he would be able to understand the circumstance in detail. If this step is skipped, insecurity regarding parents' affection and love grips the child's mind. This insecurity in turn gives rise to emotions like fear, sorrow, hatred and shock. These emotions create a turmoil in the child's mind. In that particular stage, the child becomes ready to do anything to regain the parents' interest and affection.

If these emotions of the child are not addressed appropriately, then over time, it changes to sibling rivalry. If the child was mentally prepared about the baby-to-come, this kind of adverse situations could have been averted. This particular topic was portrayed in a beautiful and sensible way in actor Surya's Tamil movie- Uyirile Kalandadu.

Children visualise even small things in a large way. Sibling rivalry, if not addressed properly during childhood, might become huge and deeply ingrained in their minds by the time they grow up. The message propagated by that movie is the closest to the reality. The boy described in the above events had disturbed feelings, and emotions like jealousy and anger took over his mind due to insecurity. This was the main reason he could not accept his baby sister.

The boy had been feeling inadequacy in the affections and attention of his parents even before his sister was born. It is just that his issues intensified with the birth of his sibling. The child was made to take several sessions of psychotherapy. This was essential to stabilize his mind and thoughts. This was achieved in several sessions of art therapy, play therapy and story-telling sessions. Sibling rivalry can be managed only with love and through patience.

The parents too, were offered counselling. They were made to understand that before every change, preparing the kids mentally for that particular change is necessary. The situation like the one described in the events, could have been averted. Even most adults find it staggeringly difficult to adapt to new situations. So, how can the children be any exceptions?

Currently, the boy is in 6th standard. He has evolved quite well after the sessions with the counsellor. He has mentally and emotionally accepted his sister and he even defends her in several situations. The parents' changed behaviour and loving attitude has propelled the boy towards a better mental stability and attitude. It has affected his growth positively.

THOUGHTS:

When a woman is pregnant, her thoughts and feelings have a deep impact on her unborn child. It is believed that if the mother has negative emotions and feelings, the baby will imbibe those feelings. This will be evident only later in life. Till the child is about 3years of age, it is considered as the foundation period for the child's mentality and personality development. This period has an everlasting influence on the child's personality, into adolescence.

When we compare ourself with others, we tend to develop feelings of jealousy. Hurting self with such averse feelings is not advisable. Jealousy is the root cause of anger and sadness. The moods and emotions we absorb and internalize, affects our personality. There are lot of activities happening around us. We often get to know about them all only through media. But, we all know that we cannot accept all of it to be pure truth. Whichever is selected and accepted by us to be the truth, our growth story will be according to it. Patience is positive feeling embedded in everyone. It is the exact opposite of 'jealousy'. It is essential to be aware of the feeling of jealousy, which naturally lurks in the mind of every individual.

EXERCISES:

WAYS TO DEVELOP PATIENCE:

1. Tolerating quietly is a virtue. It teaches patience, endurance and determination and helps achieve the strength of mental maturity.

2. When going to public places, make it a habit to follow the queue system, if present. It assists in increasing the virtue of patience.

3. If you get used to accepting unwanted tasks and situations, you can inculcate patience automatically.

4. Make it a point to associate yourself with the elderly, the handicapped and physically disabled individuals. You will get to see the other side of life and will learn to treat others with patience and respect.

5. If you praise and appreciate the virtues and morality of others around you, you will feel the negative emotions like jealousy disappearing within you and virtues like patience developing within.

6. If you are in a circumstance which is irreversible, try to accept it wholeheartedly.

7. We might face many obstacles, setbacks, trials and tribulations in life. However, only the virtue of patience can keep us on our track of commitment.

8. Patience is the quiet endurance of one's illness and physical disability. However, if you have patience, you will be able to tread on the path of your talents.

9. Mental pressure and depression makes our mind lose stability. Patience increases our mental power and stabilizes our mind.

10. If you embrace your physical and natural abilities with a smile, your journey towards your growth will make your

time worthwhile.

CHAPTER FIFTEEN

UNDERSTANDING AND SEPARATION

FOR ANY RELATION TO BE SUCCESSFUL, LOVING CONVERSATIONS, MUTUAL UNDERSTANDING AND APPRECIATION ARE ESSENTIAL. ------ MIRANDA KERR

Nowadays, most problems in our society are caused by misunderstandings, be it at home, workplace or relationships. It's an issue faced by the educated and the illiterates and the rich and the poor alike. Pride and arrogance of self are the main barriers to accept others' opinions or even understand the other person.

EVENTS:

There was a family of four. The father was a businessman. The mother was a homemaker and used to manage the household with great love and care. Their elder daughter was in 1st year of college and the younger son was in 8th standard in school. The daughter was an intelligent academician and was gifted at poetry. She would often write for her college magazine and participated in many poetry competitions and won. But she was more of an introvert. She would have a really difficult time socializing and did not mingle with her fellow students. She did not have any long term friends because she would never adjust herself for anyone, be it at home or at college. Her classmates knew well that she would approach them only in case of any necessity. However, her brother would bring his friends over to home and would have fun. The siblings would often bicker about this issue. The boy, however, on the advice of their mother, would lay down on the argument with his sister even though he wasn't at fault. But, the girl would be stubborn and expect others to do her bidding. In case the others did not, she would even quit talking to them. The parents knew this about her but did not mind much thinking that with time, she would understand things.

From the second month of college, she had trouble. She would come home every day with a resentful mind after having difference of opinion with her classmates. Finding faults with people was a never ending phenomenon. Then she would behave as if she was a perfect person and had nothing to change about herself. If she approached her fellow class mates when they were engrossed in some discussion, they would just answer out of courtesy and then continue with their conversations. They would not be keen on involving her into their chats. Her fellow mates did not look forward to going with outings with her. Thus feeling dejected, she would lament about the same to her mother. She would get into severe brawls with her brother as well. Out of anger, she would even break things at home. Eventually, she ascertained that the college in which she was studying wasn't good enough. It was evident that she wasn't interested at all in going to college. She was just dragging herself to college every day. Soon, she started taking leaves often. She could not even sleep properly and became an insomniac. Seeing all these changes in her, the concerned parents visited me with her.

QUESTIONS:

1. What was the reason the girl could not adjust with her fellow students and other people?
2. Why was the girl not accepted into her friends' circle even though she was intelligent and talented?
3. What was the reason behind her breaking the household items?

DESCRIPTION:

The student described in the above events could not accommodate with her fellow students and others due to lack of tolerance and low patience levels. Since a very young age, the parents were quite lenient and too affectionate. This exactly has caused the current situation. Although the girl was intelligent and was gifted with exceptional poetry skills, she wasn't popular with her class mates. This can be attributed to her being inconsistent and stubbornly expecting others to do her bidding. This created a distance between her and others at her college.

The young people of today's generation prefer sharing their mind, ideas and thoughts with their peers rather than with family. So, when this option wasn't available for her, she felt rejected and could not accept it. This frustration morphed into anger and as a whole, she had a nervous breakdown. As a result of which, she started breaking household items. Usually when one is rejected or denied, he/she would be offended. The wounds of frustration and rejection weigh heavy on mind and often manifest in various ways in different individuals.

The girl was offered psychological counselling through several sessions. She was emphasized on the point that only if she steps out of her comfort zone, can she resolve her complications. Gradually, over several sessions, she was explained this point and was encouraged to bring about a change in her personality.

Her parents too were offered counselling regarding how to regulate their actions. They implemented the knowledge acquired in the sessions at home. They encouraged their daughter to use her intellect in the right way and propelled her gifted talent of poetry into the direction which will benefit her in the future.

Finally, after multiple sessions, she attended the same college and even topped the university. She made her mark in the college. The happy parents shared her success story with me jubilantly.

THOUGHTS:

The biggest accusation that the children and youth make nowadays, is that their parents never understood them. When a person's needs are not met, their enigma expands and ultimately leaves them astray. There may be several reasons as to why a person lives through misunderstandings. For example, with the issue of valuing others, imaginative situations, expectations, unfinished desires etc., most of these go unnoticed. Most parents nowadays, knowingly or unknowingly aren't emphasizing on raising their children to be ideal humans.

In today's world, the focus of the child is mostly on devices like smart phones and social media. This has led to rifts in relationships and friction between family members. Children who grow up in the shadow of their parents, grow up to be anxious and timid individuals and suffer later in life from uncertainty and not being able to take appropriate decisions. Being entirely dependent on parents, they find it difficult to come out of their comfort zone to do something by themselves. When children learn to live with many types of people in a society, they get more first-hand experience regarding human relationships. This experience enriches their personality and helps them thrive when they grow up to be independent individuals.

EXERCISES:

INSTRUCTIONS FOR UNDERSTANDING CHILDREN:

1. It is natural to have a difference of opinion between people in various kinds of relationships. However, if you try to see through their point and learn to respect others opinions gracefully, there is a fair chance of building trustworthy relationships.

2. Bear clean and idealistic thoughts with an open mind. This is necessary in maintaining relationships.

3. Whenever you express your ideas or feelings, you should take care that your words are not defamatory to anyone or maligning anyone in the society. It is necessary to respect your peers opinions and then, gracefully acknowledge your line of thought.

4. In any event, do not be bent upon finding faults in others. Never resort to defaming someone. Instead, try to reason their behaviour or act. This might give you more understanding regarding the person.

5. We must always bear in mind that our thoughts and words should target only the issue to be tackled, not the individual. This is an important aspect in maintaining relations.

6. When a problem arises, criticizing the individual or situation won't solve anything. Instead, try encouraging the person by appreciating or highlighting his/her talents.

7. In a relationship, acknowledge your feelings and desires in an open minded way and firmly. Suppressing emotions won't do any good.

8. If you want to develop the skill of understanding in relationships, learn to listen keenly and wholeheartedly to what the other person is speaking.

9. Often, we can make out a lot of details about a person of interest merely by observe their body-language and actions keenly. But, if sometimes, we fail to understand as such, then there is nothing wrong in communicating with them directly and getting clarified .

10. As we all know, misunderstandings are the root cause of unwanted problems in human relationships. It's not desirable to give up on someone merely based on misunderstandings. Hence, trying to realign our thoughts and giving up our ego is the right way to go!

PART - 4 (HABITS)

If you inculcate the right habits, you can strike any ambition of yours.---- Napolean Hill

CHAPTER SIXTEEN

DIFFERENCES BETWEEN ENCOURAGEMENTS AND DISCOURAGEMENTS

Even if you criticize a person, it should feel like rain. Just the way rain doesn't damage the roots, but helps the plant thrive, your criticism should provide the necessary motivation to grow. - Frank Clark

Encouragement is definitely an emotion which stirs up an agenda within us. It compels us to develop an interest to complete a task. Being invisible to the naked eye, victory is a primary trait embedded in each person. But, it can be attained only by endeavouring for it. In a life devoid of motivation, there would not be any interest towards studies, job, income or savings either. It is an established fact that self-encouragement works as a more intense driving force than external encouragement.

EVENTS:

There lived a family of five, father mother and their three sons. The eldest son was in 10th standard. The second son was in 7th standard and the youngest one was in 3rd standard. They were all brilliant in academics. Each of them were talented and gifted in different ways. The elder son was ever ready to help out in case of any requirement in the household. He was a responsible person and was thus, often entrusted with any small errands of the household. The youngest son was the star kid of the household and was the centre of everyone's attention. The second son often felt, "Whatever I do or achieve , my parents do not give me any attention at all,". Due to this kind of thoughts, his academics and his other activities took a plunge. The thoughts of being neglected by his parents got deep rooted into his mind and he reduced his interactions with others. He compared himself with others and feelings of inferiority complex gripped his mind. He felt that even his presence at home was usually being unnoticed. He suffered from lack of appetite. When this behaviour of his intensified, the concerned parents came to meet me with him.

QUESTIONS TO PONDER UPON FROM THE ABOVE EVENTS:

1. What kind of thoughts would be going on in the boy's (second son) mind?
2. What was the reason for his setback in the academics?
3. Did the parents observe a change in the boy's behaviour early on?

DESCRIPTION:

The boy had thoughts like, " I'm not getting the same amount of affection and importance that my brothers are enjoying. May be our parents do not like me anymore. That's why they are not as much concerned about me as they are about my brothers". Innumerable thoughts like these were rallying his mind. This kind of neglect from his parents left him heart broken. When so many thoughts were going on in his mind, he would often seem dull and tired. His pale demeanour often suggested that he lost something valuable. Contemplating on these kind of thoughts, he began comparing self with his brothers and others. Gradually, he developed self-hate and inferiority complex about himself. This became the prime reason for the setback in his academics and normal life.

The parents noticed the changes behaviour of their son and understood that something was wrong with him. But they did not know what that was in particular. His day to day life and activities were so weird that his mental disturbance was evident to his parents. They recognized the need for an external help for their son.

I sat him down. In the initial interaction, I tried to instil faith in him and to change his line of thought. Psychotherapy pacified his notions about his family and helped him reason his beliefs.

Then, the parents were counselled on how to help their son from his current state and how to encourage him enough so that he starts regaining confidence in them and, more importantly, in himself.

He was nudged consistently with love and care by his parents. His achievements were emphasised on and were appreciated openly. This changed attitude of the parents brought about a lot of changes in his personality.

In the last three years, his decision making skills and his self-confidence while withstanding failures left his parents bewildered and overjoyed. Currently he is in 11th. He is now able to decide concretely about which course he wants to take up, the college he wants to join and the career he wants to make. He now aims precisely and works diligently towards it.

THOUGHTS:

Parents are the first people to provide their child with motivation and propelling their child towards achievements. This motivation is the exact thing that goes a long way with the child into his/her future. When teachers provide encouragement, it boosts the child's learning capacity. When your leader or boss appreciates and encourages you, you tend to discover more about yourself and your talents.

If children are not used to facing challenges while growing up, as adults, they would struggle to do the same. Children must get used to 'no' as an answer. Parents must abstain from buying their children unnecessary things. Children must learn to differentiate between needs and desires, at least on a small scale. They should get used to having minor conflicts with peers. Only then can they learn how to deal with the emotions associated with that and how to deal with circumstances like that. Encourage and motivate your children to take up challenges and difficult tasks (according to their age, of course!).

The minute details in a relationship can be realised only when interacting with people. This realization will shine on us. Trusting others and providing appropriate encouragement is necessary both to attain success and to retain the success.

When it comes to children, giving them appropriate suggestions provides more encouragement than giving them advices. Utilizing the power of self-encouragement enables you to hit the bull's eye. Even though one possess talent and skills, if they do not keep themselves motivated, they wouldn't see the horizons of success.Today, most people in our society are in dire need of a friend who can encourage you after a failure rather than a person who appreciates you after a success.

EXERCISES:

WAYS TO MOTIVATE CHILDREN:

1. Encouragement is an emotion which stirs up an agenda within ourselves. Take care to never let the motivation lose the flame.
2. We ought to surround ourselves with people who would encourage us with gallant ideas and with their trust.
3. When your child tells you something, even if you respond with just a 'yes', it itself will be a great

encouragement for them. Then, they will start sharing every piece of their mind with you.

4. When it comes to children, a profound motivation after a failure is more important than an appreciation after a success.

5. Instead of advising, try suggesting. Let your children choose or determine an appropriate solution from your suggestions.

6. Teach your children to take criticism the right way. It should not be taken to heart or in an emotional way. Rather, take it as encouragement. A motivational talk. Only then, can it become your strength.

7. Competition determines the thin line between failure or victory. If you encounter failure, do not become grim and dull. Instead, work up a come-back plan and step ahead with all your might.

8. Teach some fun tips to children about team work and the responsibilities associated with it. Guide them into good behaviour and give them a detailed explanation about how team work actually pays off.

9. Teach your children how to handle tensions and mental pressure. Acknowledge the fact that failing to achieve something will not mean it is the end of the world. This fact must be embedded firmly in their young minds.

10. Motivate your children to find a field of their interest and to make an aim. Pave the way for them to realise their ambition. As parents, you must be able to provide them with the necessary motivation and opportunities.

CHAPTER SEVENTEEN

APPRECIATION AND SHARING

If you cherish and respect others, you will get the same in return.----Poet Kannadasan.

Sharing is the ability to give a part of whatever we have to others. But it does not mean we expect the same in return. Sharing is a virtue which wins over selfishness. When we share something without a selfish intent, we unconsciously change ourselves for the better. As human beings, we are equipped with an inborn quality of generosity and sharing.Well, let us admit to ourselves that we actually crave appreciation in some or the other way. It's a natural trait in us humans. But, most people just do not value others openly. When you start appreciating the small things about others around you, the envy and jealousy gripped in your mind starts waning. Gradually, you start to build good relationships around you.When children are introduced to the quality of sharing, they automatically learn the quality of appreciating. They will start sharing things around just to gain some appreciation. They will realise that magnanimity is an appreciable trait.

EVENTS:

There lived a family of three, the father, mother and their daughter. The father was an engineer on a ship. The mother was an accountant in a bank. The daughter had completed college and was awaiting marriage. The parents were in search of a suitable groom for her. The mother was extremely upset about a particular behaviour pattern of her daughter and not knowing how to tackle the issue, met me regarding it. I'm summarizing a part of the events as described to me by the mother.

The daughter was a clever girl was gifted in several ways. She would even top her class in academics. But, since her school days, her mother had been hearing the same complaint about her from multiple people, many times.

It was a habit about her. She did not like sharing even small things with anyone or wouldn't help anyone around her even with small things. She did not know something called generosity. The mother thought that this habit of hers would fade with time as she grows. She would realise the importance of sharing with age. So she didn't not mind all that much. Then, one day, when she was in college, her professor shared an incident with her mother. Everyone in the college knew that the girl habitually carried an umbrella with her. One day, when it was pouring heavily, the professor was unable to get into the auto from his staffroom. So he asked the girl to share her umbrella temporarily, so that he can reach his auto-rickshaw. But, to his surprise, she refused.

In this way, she would have to do a lot of thought work even to extend a small help. She was indeed facing a problem trusting others.In another event, the girl's aunt i.e her mother's younger sister visited them. The aunt had finalized a groom for her daughter. The groom and his family were going to visit them the following evening. So she requested her elder sister to let her borrow a piece of jewellery, at least a chain for her daughter, the reason being her own jewellery was mortgaged in the bank. She assured that she would return the chain after the groom's family left. The daughter being described in the events above, was keenly listening to the conversation. Her sudden and impudent reply startled both her mother and her aunt. She barbarously asked her aunt to get her daughter married with whatever they had. She made it clear that she wasn't keen on sharing her jewellery even temporarily. Her reply reflected her extreme pride and arrogance. Her aunt was mortified at her outrage and left for her house in tears.

The mother was equally shocked at what just happened and regretted not correcting her behaviour earlier. She indeed did not have even a speck of the virtue of sharing. The mother realised that her waiting that the daughter would change with age was in vain. She felt that it was too late for her to try to do something. So, before getting her daughter married, she wanted to get her counselled about how small incidents of generosity can be important in maintaining relationships. She wanted her daughter to understand how sharing genuinely can develop new relations. She sought the suggestions of a psychologist for this issue.

QUESTIONS TO PONDER UPON FROM THE ABOVE EVENTS:

1. Why did the girl could not develop have the virtue of sharing?
2. Did the parents delay too much in correcting her? Has this delay affected her too bad?

DESCRIPTION:

If you examine the actual problem of the girl described in the above events minutely, you will find the root of it in her childhood. Her mother, who was an accountant in a bank, had to re-join her job just when the girl was 1 month old. The girl could be breast -fed for only a month. Then, to look after the baby, they had appointed a babysitter. The baby sitter was quite close-fisted and a miserly person by nature. Since the baby was closely associated with her and as it is babies' nature to unconsciously absorb whatever is there in their surroundings, she naturally imbibed the stingy nature from her. The distance from the mother at such a young age definitely impacted her emotions . She developed feelings of insecurity.

According to psychologists, the first three years of growth of a child is crucial. The child is like a sponge, imbibing every emotion surrounding him/her. These emotions shape up their personality and character. This however reveals itself in various ways, only later in life.

Now, you might have understood the source of her habit of stinginess and unwillingness to share. It is an established fact that the environment influences around 50% of personality. The other 50% of personality, nature and character development comes from parents. If the parents had taken note of this nature of hers in the childhood, it would have been easy to curb this. But delay in recognising the problem itself has created the current havoc in both the parents and the daughter's life.

It has become evident now, that during the childhood, she did not feel assured and secure. The parents should have created an environment of assurance and should have taken steps to induce a sense of security and comfort to her as a baby. Instead, the estrangement of the mother and child during infancy and the deprived intimacy with the mother through breast-feeding has generated feelings of fear and insecurity in the child's mind. These feelings gripped the child's mind, further creating feelings of unfaithfulness. These emotions have created a personality about her by which she would take care of her things with extreme possessiveness so as not to be estranged from them. She would feel insecure and apprehensive in case of losing some belonging of hers. This kind of thought deprived her of developing the virtue of sharing. She failed to realise that only by sharing can she receive appreciation and achieve genuine friendship with others.

The parents were counselled in multiple sessions. They were advised about how to deal with their adolescent daughter and how to willingly expose her to her friends and neighbours. They were suggested to visit places like an orphanage or an old age home as a family and do some service there to express thankfulness. This act will indirectly plant the virtue of sharing in her mind and will encourage her to be generous to others.Next, the girl was offered counselling in multiple sessions. A type of treatment called 'Healing the inner child' was used to treat the feelings of distrust embedded in the child's mind. Psychotherapy was used to change her line of thought and her feelings of insecurity was gradually tried to be erased. Knowing about the girl's mind in detail, with continuous treatment, her thoughts and personality was changed. After an year of psychological treatment, a difference in her attitude and behaviour was evident.

Recently, she got married and was quite happy in her family life. Her parents were content about their daughter's life. This meeting was a turning point in life for the daughter. She went on to post graduate in Social Sciences and has decided to make a career in Social work to serve her community.

THOUGHTS:

There would be no one on this planet who wouldn't like appreciation and praise. It acts as a driving force to move forward in life. When you appreciate others, the situations around you will change for the better. People around you at office, society or even family will become ever friendly to you. Appreciation encourages love. When you appreciate someone, you express your love for them. Appreciation builds value and helps gain respect from others. When you appreciate someone's efforts, you are expressing your affection for them. Appreciation invokes value and respect. If you keep appreciating someone, you are respecting and valuing their work. If people start respecting each other, their relationship evolves in a beautiful manner. If parents practice generosity, their children will watch and learn the same. They will develop the habit of sharing , will gain friendship and trust of peers and will learn to love and respect others. These emotions play well within them to shape their personality and paves way for growing up into a good human being. Explaining a mature person about the importance of sharing is difficult. But explaining and teaching the same to children, step by step, gradually, every day, continuously can help them imbibe the true spirit of generosity.

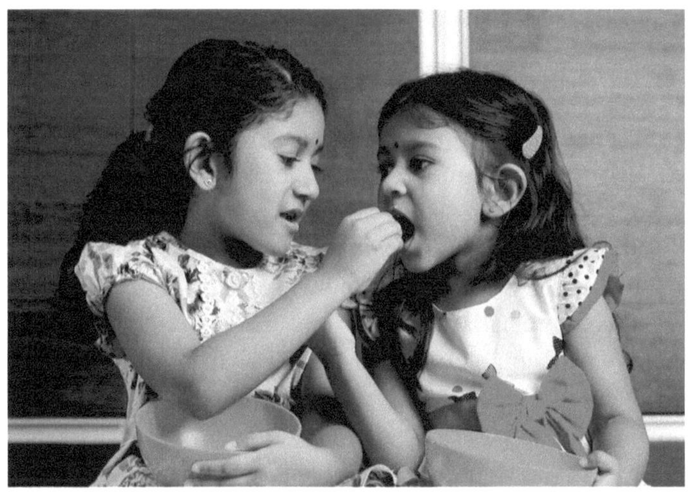

EXERCISES:
WAYS TO TEACH THE IMPORTANCE OF SHARING TO CHILDREN:

1. When children are taught the art of sharing, they automatically develop the quality of appreciating.

2. It is a proven fact that children follow what we do rather than what we say. When we practise generosity in front of children, they watch and will learn the same.

3. In today's generation, rather than sharing finances, sharing your knowledge learned through your experience can be a more useful. Beyond materialistic help, sharing ideas can help others grow.

4. When sharing some of their belongings, children can feel the joy of giving. For example, have them participate when donating at orphanage, nursing home or an old age home.

5. Spending your time on useful things for others is also a kind of sharing.

6. Identify the things you have in excess, like clothes, books, stationary, gifts. Share them with people in need. This might help the receivers with something necessary.

7. When you compliment others wholeheartedly, envy and jealousy recedes and helps strengthen your relationship.

8. Praise is the way to express love. If you value yourself and others, your affection will be expressed through your appreciation.

9. A small compliment to a child will give them great encouragement. Support them and help them handle their life more creatively.

10. When you appreciate someone, you are helping them build their self-confidence. Your compliments can make the person feel strong.

CHAPTER EIGHTEEN

GADGETS CAN ACT AS A CONNECTION BETWEEN PARENT AND CHILD

BEING EXEMPLARY ISN'T THE FIRST WAY TO SET ONESELF ABOVE OTHERS. THAT IS THE ONLY WAY. — ALBERT EINSTEIN

Nowadays, electronic devices have become a part and parcel of every household. It is impossible to imagine a life without them. Children have become kind of addicted to devices. The impact of it is a damaged relationship between parent and child. Children are bonding with and spending more time with these devices rather than with parents or relatives. Both the physical and mental health of children and adults are being negatively affected by these devices.

EVENTS:

There was a family of four. The father was a businessman. The mother was a home maker. They had two children. The elder one, their daughter was mentally ill. The younger son was in 10th class now. Till he was in 9th class, his daily routine after school was having his tea, doing his homework and going to his tuition (special class). On returning from his tuition, he would interact with his sister for a while and then would go to sleep. By the time he entered 10th class, he repeatedly requested his parents to buy a smartphone. Then he started being adamant about the same. Not being able to withstand his stubbornness, they finally bought him one. But then, his academics took a setback. He started playing games on his cell phone and became kind of addicted to them. He was enjoying himself thoroughly with his smartphone. He would experience anxiety when distancing himself from it. He would become angry if he could not find it anywhere near himself. He would feel frustrated and scream with annoyance in case he did not find it where he had kept. He would even become violent at times. The parents were troubled at his behaviour and said that they bought him the device even though they knew it wouldn't help him much.

QUESTIONS TO PONDER OVER FROM THE ABOVE EVENTS:

1. What was the reason the son spent so much time on the cell phone?
2. Why was the boy plunged into this state?

DESCRIPTION:

If you probe into the boy's problem deeply, you can observe that he wasn't allowed to play outdoors with his friends. How much time could he talk to his sister alone. At school, most of his friends were using electronic devices and discussing about various things related to them. But, he could not follow them because did not know anything about the devices at all. He would feel anxious about having no knowledge about it. Sometimes he would even feel left out and angry about not being able to know about it. As a typical teenager, he adamantly asked for a cell phone and made his parents buy him one. Soon enough, he learnt playing PUBG and started creating YouTube videos.

He was trying to earn through it. Gradually, he got so addicted that his physical condition began to deteriorate. He became an insomniac, with red eyes and heavy dark circles around his eyes. His health began to worsen by each day, much without his notice at all. His full concentration was on his smart phone. His academics started declining. Even without his own awareness, his health was deteriorating day by day. It was evident that he had become an addict to mobile games. The reason behind his current state could be him obtaining a smart phone while he was still in school. The next biggest reason could be that he was given a separate room, where he was too free to use the device as and when he wanted, ithout any parental controls. All this together spelled trouble for both the parents and their son.

During the counselling session with the parents, they were explained that their continuous effort and help would be very much needed for their son to break out of his addiction. The alternative for this kind of problem would be go according to the boy's wishes but simultaneously encouraging and incentivising him to play outdoors. This will decrease the screen time considerably. The parents were also taught about using parental controls to regulate his screen time. They were advised to help the child to develop a new good habit into his daily routine and to create alternative ways to change/replace his existing habit. If he practiced his newly learned good habit for long time, it would be ingrained into his personality. He can thus distract himself from his existing smartphone addiction.

In the counselling sessions with the boy, he was highlighted the impact of smartphones on the brain and how it affects our habits and personality. He was explained that it is possible to experience severe physical and psychological damage when the addiction reaches its peak. When the boy was made aware of these facts, a change in his line of thought was evident. He started to reduce his screen usage voluntarily, little by little. He gradually overcame his addiction. His self-control has shown significant progress in an year. He is now in 11th standard, majoring in Computer Science. He is using his screen time effectively in a useful way to learn and create new ideas.

THOUGHTS:

Children nowadays prefer to be around people who allow them to use smartphones rather than people who treat them affectionately. Children who used to run around and play outdoors, now prefer watching screens. It has become rare for them to leave their house and look outdoors.

A bitter truth is that there has been a recent increase in the number of children showing up at hospitals, complaining of back pain. These children are so young that they have not even started going to school. Sitting motionless at a place for many hours watching screens is to be blamed for this. Lack of physical activity has led to juvenile obesity and severe eye problems in young children. They are even less likely to interact with others and display shyness when contacted. They are unable to maintain eye contact with people during conversations. They find it difficult to express themselves to others and thus shy away from socialising. They are unable to find appropriate words and form sentences to express what they are going through or what they are feeling. However, it isn't wise to keep our children totally away from devices. After all, everything has its pros and cons. The parents today need to learn to use parental controls and regulate the usage of the devices. Parents need to limit children's screen time and designate a few hours in a day for watching. Additionally, parents need to spend adequate quality time with their little ones. This will distract their attention from those devices.

SYMPTOMS OF ADDICTION TO ELECTRONIC DEVICES:

- Children not agreeing to playing or interacting with others without their devices.
- Even though their physical growth is normal according to their age, they would not be able to speak or express themselves fluently.
- Distancing them from devices induces frustration and anger.
- You would find them continuously browsing the internet. Even though they have nothing specific to search for, they keep on scrolling through their screens.
- Their academics take a serious setback. They lose interest in academics and learning. Not paying enough attention to their studies, they would not score enough even to get through their examinations.

EXERCISES:

HOW TO REGULATE ELECTRONIC DEVICES WITH CHILD:

1. Electronic devices cannot be kept away from children forever. After all, we all need the devices for various useful functions. So, regulating their usage by using

parental controls and limiting their screen time would be a wise way to go.

2. Introduce children to extracurricular activities like art, crafts and hobbies. Try to create an interest on a specific hobby and indulge with them.

3. Buy the electronic devices only which are necessary. Hold meaningful discussions within family and talk about the importance of relationships in the presence of children.

4. When children return home to their parents, they often have a lot to share and reveal about their time at school or park. At such time, do not ignore them. If you do, you distance yourself from them. Try to develop a close knit relationship with your children. Only then will they feel secure and safe.

5. When children come up to you to share their ideas or thoughts or experiences, as parents, we ought to pay some attention to whatever they want to say. If we deprive them of that listening ear, they would go searching for that attention somewhere else, which nowadays, is mostly over social media.

6. Encourage children to play outdoors. Introduce them to outdoor sports. This does help a lot to decrease their screen time.

7. If you find children using devices unnecessarily, try diverting their attention towards art, hobby so play. Help them get creative till they get the hang of it.

8. Try to take some time off your schedule to spend some quality time with your children. Try to do it as often as possible. With close parental interaction, they won't be much dependent on electronic devices.

9. It is a proven fact that devices hamper with our sleep quality. Deprivation of sufficient and quality sleep has

deleterious effects on health and gives rise to bad conduct. Hence, make it a point not to carry your devices to your bedroom.

10. Parents gifting electronic devices to their children is like placing the world on their palms. With these devices, the world has indeed become smaller. So, let the children understand clearly that the future of their life will purely depend on how they are handling their current situations and dealing with their challenges.

CHAPTER NINETEEN

STRUGGLING FOR ADAPTATION

BE THE CHANGE WHICH YOU DESIRE TO SEE AROUND YOU. ---- BARACK OBAMA

Children tend to accept changes little by little.However, if they encounter changes continuously, their individuality is bound to be suppressed, and with time, will develop inferiority complex. They look down upon themselves for not being able to do several normal things. When a change of location happens, even adults take some time to accommodate. Children ,hence are not exceptions for that. It is the responsibility of the adults to prepare children mentally beforehand. Otherwise, the situations might become chaotic for both children and adults.

EVENTS

There lived a family of three. The father was working in a private firm and held a high position in his office. The mother was a homemaker. She managed her household and took good care of her children. Their daughter was in 6th standard. She was a gifted artist. Her exceptionally beautiful art was applauded by many. She would participate in several competitions and won several prizes. Her father's job involved several transfers. Once in 3 years, he had to have a transfer to a different state. In the same way, this time, he was transferred to Tamil Nadu. It has been 6 months now. The previous transfers did not affect her much. But this time was quite different. She would get particularly irritated and stubborn on certain issues. She would achieve her needs by creating a hue and cry often. She would follow her parents everywhere as if she was somewhat mentally insecure. She would not interact with anyone at school and would stay aloof. Her teachers often reported about her getting into frequent brawls with her classmates. She had never exhibited this kind of behaviour previously. Seeing her deportment, and being unable to understand the reason behind it, the parents met me with their daughter.

QUESTIONS

1. Did the child accept the change of place and come to her normal behavioural situation ?
2. What was the barrier for the child to behave as usual in the new location?

DESCRIPTION:

Let us probe into the situation of the girl described in the above events in detail. She had accepted the changes in her life till she was in 5th standard. However, when she started her 6th standard, the changes she faced were different. Previously, knowingly or unknowingly, the parents had prepared her well mentally about their impending transfers. They used to convey the change of situation to her at least prior to 3 months. Whenever the parents used to socialise, at events or in the neighbourhood, they used to talk about their impending transfers and other issues. The girl used to listen to all of that and would understand the same. It would gradually be embedded in her mind. So, when they actually had to leave the place, leaving behind her friends and the locality she knew, she would miss them for sometime, but would ultimately recover soon enough without much fuss. But this time, it did not happen so. She could not accept herself in the new place and school. The reason can be attributed to the lack of mental preparation. The transfer to the current place meant a stark change in the locality, the people around and the school. Since she wasn't prepared for it psychologically, this came as a shock. There was a lot of difference in her routine life at the new place. Moreover, she was in middle school now and her syllabus too seemed a bit difficult for her. She even found her teachers to be new and had difficulty adapting to them. It took some months for her to understand all this and to accommodate in this new environment. But even before she could realise it, she had to face her exam and soon enough, her marks list too. And, as expected in her circumstance, her marks list too seemed to accuse her. She saw happy students around her gleefully chatting with each other, but she would be sad that she did not have any friends to talk to. She would reminisce about her old locality and school and felt lonely. She missed her old town and friends. Separating from the old place made her sad. All these emotions summed up into mental and physical irritation.

As she was growing up, physiological changes stirred up within her. Soon enough, she hit puberty. Her emotions and hormones ravaged her mind altogether. The parents remembered the counselling sessions which they were given around 4 months ago and shared the same with me.

The parents were given some counselling sessions on how to handle teenagers and how to prepare the child mentally for an impending change. Then, the girl was offered psychotherapy about how to accept changes in any given new place. She was explained the importance of concentration in academics and communicating with peers in school. She was given step by step tips on how to deal with the situations around her. Gradually, she started mingling with her new classmates at school. Soon, her classmates turned into her friends! She began maintaining good friendship and became quite intimate with them. She is now studying in 8th class in the same school. She participates in many drawing competitions and wins prizes too. Her parents had shared the story of her well-being with me.

THOUGHTS:

From a psychological standpoint, the developmental changes of each child takes place in almost five stages. The first stage is from birth to one year. The second stage is from one to three years. The third stage is from four to seven years. The fourth stage is from eight to twelve years. And the fifth stage is from thirteen to sixteen years.

During each stage, the developmental changes are evident in the child. From the moment a baby is born, through the time he/she develops, many experiences are gained with various situations and people. The various problems encountered by the child in life shapes up the personality and promotes their mental growth.

When it comes to a new home, new place or a new school, children, just like adults, find it somewhat challenging to accommodate. Beyond all of this and most importantly, the other thing which affects children is the friends circle. Emotional turmoil created from new places and encountering new people shows up as stubbornness and weeping over unnecessary things. They even resort to hurling and flinging of various things around them. The reason for this kind of anger is that children express their emotions through actions rather than words. Different kinds of confusions appear in the child's mind. These confusions gives rise to a dilemma in the child's mind.

EXERCISES:

WAYS FOR CHILDREN TO ADAPT TO CHANGES:

1. By exposing children to new changes often from an early age, they will be encouraged to accept the new circumstances in future.

2. When someone tries to bring about a change in themselves, they do tend to take some time to jump from their old habits to their new ones. In that case, try to give a little break from the situation. Let the children see the development.

3. Once you step out of your comfort zone, you will encounter changes faster than usual.

4. When you turn your life events to your experiences, your growth story will have much less struggle incidents recorded in it.

5. You may encounter many undesirable changes in your life. But, you should understand that there may be some hidden opportunities within them. Depending on how you decide to face it or deal with it, it will lead you on the path of development.

6. It is important to value the opinion of others. While doing so, take care not to hurt the unique identity or the individuality of others and yourself.

7. When a person is emotionally attached to a certain place, it will be a struggle for him to move to somewhere else. If this emotion is not overcome, it will become an obstacle in the path of their progress.

8. If you want to progress, you need to change. It is imperative to bring your mind to a stable state of readiness.

9. Allow yourself to face the challenges life has to offer you. You cannot achieve anything in life without confronting the test of time and circumstance.

10. The only thing that does not change in life is Change. It's unavoidable. Hence, it would be wise to accept it and use it to climb the ladders of success.

CHAPTER TWENTY

DIFFERENCES BETWEEN ADVICE AND COUNSELLING

THERE ARE THREE WAYS TO ACHIEVE SOMETHING IN LIFE. TRY TO KNOW MORE THAN OTHERS, LEARN TO WORK HARDER THAN OTHERS AND TRY TO HOLD LESS DEBT COMPARED TO OTHERS. — WILLIAM SHAKESPEARE.

In today's civilised and developed world, it is becoming more and more challenging to spend time with family and children. Talking to family privately or spending some quality time privately has become tough. The prime necessity for children in life is love, support and protection. A single lid cannot fit correctly on jars of all sizes. In the same way, there cannot be a single solution to all the problems of children. Counselling must be tailored to the nature of the problem, to suit the child's mental state and comfort, his/her family situation, intelligence and personality development.

EVENTS:

There was a family of four, a father, mother, their daughter and son. The daughter was studying in the 3rd year in a college. The son was studying in the 12th standard. It had come to the parents' attention that since some months, their son wasn't at his best behaviour. He would come home late after roaming around with his friends. His derelict behaviour had been criticised. Many a time, arguments would crop up because of many of his disorderly conduct, like him being obsessed with smartphones and the ridiculous usage of electronic devices .

However, the parents did not take all of this seriously. Even when some of their relatives and friends expressed their concern about his activities, they did not mind about it much. One day, he was returning home late as usual. At the same, the police were chasing someone on the same road he and his friends were walking on. The police felt that these boys could serve as an eyewitness to something they were searching about and hence, brought them all to the police station for the night. They started conducting an enquiry and questioned them if they had seen someone running on the road. The boys were even questioned about the reason they were roaming the streets at such a late hour.

That day, he couldn't reach home. His parents were obviously quite worried and were continually searching for him. The following morning, they received a call from the police station. They were informed about the entire incident and were asked to reprimand their son. Everyone in the house was shocked to know that he was in the police station all night. Two days after the incident, the parents had come to see me with their son.

QUESTIONS TO PONDER UPON FROM THE ABOVE EVENTS:

1. What is the role of the family to push the boy into such a state?
2. Why did the parents not bother about their son and did not guide him properly at that age?

DESCRIPTION:

One of the main reasons behind the current situation of the boy described in the above events is his family . Since a very young age , the parents have limited themselves to just advising the boy. Neither did they mind much about his habits nor did they reprimand him or try to correct his ways. Getting used to such light reprimands, in his current teenage, even though his parents and lot of other people are pointing out at his misdoings, he is refusing to bring about a change to his behaviour. If the parents had made small attempts to modify his line of thought and actions during his childhood, the current unpleasant situation could have been avoided.

It is a well-known fact that advice doesn't go down very well with most teenagers. They generally tend to learn from their own experiences and pitfalls or by watching peers and surroundings. Some would even follow intellectuals or some scholarly persons and imbibe their personalities, and perpetually mend their ways.

During the sessions, the parents were ascertained the importance of added attention and guidance during the teenage phase of their son. It is imperative to deal with the current generation with spontaneity and presence of mind. Next, the boy was offered some psychological counselling sessions. Soon enough, the parents were pleasantly surprised by some small changes in their son's attitude and reported the same to me. They were amazed and asked me what did I do for such a pragmatic change in their son.

So, during the sessions, firstly, the boy was pacified. He was made to reminisce his ambitions and desires. Then he was offered the necessary psychological help on how to realise his dreams. He was assisted to clear his thoughts and focus upon him achieving his aspirations. He was motivated to take an accurate decision regarding uplifting himself and implementing the same.

Normally , most teenagers follow the reverse rule, that is, they would do exactly the forbidden thing. Just by making small achievable changes in his ambitions and motivating him to follow them did the trick. Later, the boy had several sessions pacifying his turbulent waves of thoughts. He was encouraged to talk and discuss about his ideas. His line of thought was tried and turned towards a more productive path of achieving his aspirations. Thus, gradually, over a period of time, his grim conduct improved. His addiction to smart phone diminished. His late night aimless outings with his friends too reduced in frequency. He began focusing on productive ways to uplift himself.

THOUGHTS:

A very well-known but, somewhat dismal fact : Kids do not like advice. They would rather prefer suggestions. The parental ingenuity lies in making the children realise the fact that whatever they are being said is for their own benefit. Many people think that counselling is a sort of guidance that comes through experience. Like what parents impart to children or teachers impart to students. When officers advise their staff or physicians advise their patients, it can be called a 'guidance' too. But, counselling is a superior art form of psychology which helps follow action plans. This is very much a scientific practice of dealing with stages of development in humans and in their personalities. This is a form of tailored guidance for each individual to move forward in their life.

Every parent raises their children in the following four stages:

- First stage is primary guidance at 1 to 10 years old. (Directing)

- Second stage is Training at 11 to 18 years old. (Coaching)
- Third stage is the supporting level, at 19 to 24 years old. (Supporting)
- Fourth stage is imparting responsibility at 25 years old and above. (Delegating)

Kenneth Blanchard mentions these four stages in his book. Parents need to guide their children with their integrated knowledge, depending upon the age of the kid and whatever situation they are in.

EXERCISES:

WAYS TO NURTURE CHILDREN INTO GOOD CONDUCT:

1. When children are given a little break or time to realise and correct their mistakes, they will gain the maturity to accept it.
2. When your little ones do a mistake, advise them to use it as an experience rather than feeling guilty and pondering over it endlessly.
3. Children are often eager to implement whatever they see or learn new. If you show your interest in whatever they are attempting to do, that will act as an encouraging sign for them and will positively impact their self-confidence.
4. At times, your child will be obsessively interested in completing a task or a game or a thing of creativity. Never intercept his thoughts at such times. Let him follow his intellect or imagination. If you try to intercept their thoughts or define the rules of their creativity, it will definitely affect their personality later in life. Adults should not interrupt a busy child if it does not affect

them in any way.

5. When it is something regarding children, everyone in the family must be on the same line of thought. Everyone must carry the same belief about a thing if it concerns the children of their household. But, if everyone carries a different contemplation, it will confuse the child immensely about which line of thought is to be followed. In later stages, this might affect his/her personality too.

6. At times, children will be able to sense that their actions are unpleasant. At such instances, help them understand their intuition better by speaking to them privately.

7. As wrong it is to resist expressing your affections, so it is to think of controlling your children with love or force. It is necessary to realise the importance of flexibility for the appropriate growth of your child.

8. Teach your children to forgive and forget others mistakes. If you do the same with them, they will learn the art of forgiving, easily.

9. For problems that are not manageable, it is necessary to seek help of specialists or mental health counsellors.

10. For a child who grows up with a sense of independence, he will be at ease while solving his own problems. The decision-making power comes naturally, exploring the mass defects of skill and strength.

CHAPTER TWENTY-ONE

CONNECT TO CORRECT

All relationships are built on mutual trust and respect. — Mona Sutpen.

Loving human beings will always be stable and their matured minds will continue to do good without any change. Some perceive it as weakness. Love and kindness are the symbols of one's good life. We need to test our instincts to see if those signs work in us.

EVENTS:

There lived a family of three . The father was a business man, the mother was a doctor and the daughter was in the 7th grade at school. Being busy at their professional life, they could not spend much time with their child, ever since her childhood . The poor girl always kept looking forward for the love and affection of her parents. Due to lack of much interaction at home, she learned things by observing people around and by seeing her friends. So, to impress her classmates and to make them her best buddies, she would bring hard cash from her home and splurge on them. One day she took ten thousand rupees from home. For some reason, at school, the students' bags were checked as a routine. The authorities were taken aback to find such a huge amount in her school bag. On questioning, she answered that, she would bring money to school every day to spend on her friends. The headmistress called the parents and briefed them about the incident and asked them to come to school immediately to collect the cash. Furthur, her teacher supposed that she might have learnt some other unnecessary habits from around her, which they were unaware of. She even suggested that they should pay little more attention to whatever is going on in their daughter's mind. The parents left the school, but this meeting made them feel a bit insulted. Hence, unknowingly though, they look out their stress on her and started scolding her constantly and finding faults with her. After a few days, the girl retorted in anger that she did not like both of them as parents. Her words ' do not like' went deep into the parents' minds. A few days later, they visited me with their daughter.

QUESTIONS TO PONDER OVER FROM THE ABOVE EVENTS:

1. Why was the girl pushed into a situation where she wanted to take money from home?

2. What was the contribution of the parents to the activities of the child?

DESCRIPTION:

The student described in the above events was pushed to the point of taking money from home to spend it with her friends because of loneliness, her nostalgia of love and affection and her craving to belong with others. As her urge to be with her parents was not being realised, she took money from home and spent it on her friends, expecting to build a bond of affection and friendship. Thus, she formed a friend circle for herself. The parents' decreased attention towards her ever since her childhood, contributed to her activities. She was always longing for the affection of her parents. But, when she could not receive that from her parents, she stared searching for the same affection outside home . As parents, before reprimanding your child, remember C2 : CONNECT TO CORRECT. Only if you practice this rule, you would be able to see the desired change in your child's behaviour .

In the events mentioned above, when the teacher called the parents, and informed them about their daughter, they took it as an insult. Frustration caused them to show it on the child by constantly finding faults with her. This act of the parents furthur trenched their relationship with their daughter. The outcome of it, the little girl retorting and expressing dislike for her parents.

Well, as a matter of fact, we cannot say that punishing children should be totally forbidden . The pointer is that admonishing with a hint of love is necessary . When trying to correct a child, do not expect instant reformation in his/her habit of attitude. It should be done artistically, with a lot of patience and simultaneous appraisal of their good deeds. Parents must keep in mind that expressing their anger harshly will never be useful. Instead they must continue giving their unconditional love and support. This is the only way to bring about a permanent positive change in the children's attitude and personality .

In the events described above, even though the parent-child relationship was trenched, the parents needed to intercept her actions when she was wrong. But, the young child could not understand it and felt almost estranged. During the counselling sessions, the parents were made to understand that if children do not receive love since a very young age , they feel empty from within. They were made aware of the importance of parental love while raising children . They were suggested to spend quality time with their child, expressing their affection in various ways, so that the child builds a strong bond of faith and love with her parents .

The daughter was offered several sessions of therapy in which she was enlightened about how teenage sprouts various emotions within us and the risks associated with getting close to strangers. She was suggested ways to approach strangers when necessary . Currently, the girl is in 10th class. I came to know about her well-being when her parents cheerfully narrated all about her attitude and her academic performances .

THOUGHTS:

The prime duty of parents is to correct the mistakes that their children make as they grow up. Every parent naturally desires a well disciplined child. Discipline by definition, is recognized when children bring their actions under their own control. As parents, we must embed the fact well in our minds that, children's actions and behaviour cannot be controlled through violence or power. Rather, they can be changed with love and care. A child who is disciplined through violence, as they grow up, will have the thought of punishing others in his/her mind. At the same time, the children who are disciplined with love and kindness, the change will be embedded in their personality and their disciplined nature will be permanent.

According to psychologists, 80% of today's children and adults in prisons are in there, because they could not receive unconditional love and hence could not return the same to people around them. While imposing restrictions on children, try to pay attention to their comments about it. Hear out what they have to say or what they feel about implementing the rules. Take account of their wishes and if you can, try to lighten your controls or regulations a little. This little bit of leniency can act as an encouragement for them to actually follow the rules willingly. However, if you feel that it would not be right for the child, disagree gracefully. Psychological research shows that children often do not violate the decisions which are made along with their consideration. Relationships are bound by love and affection. It takes a lot of work and understanding for an individual to suit the person they love. In modern times, homes have shrunk and so have the relationships. And along with it, even the fondness for one another has diminished. Hence, in these modern times, more important than ever, the loving and comprehensible guidance of parents to lead their children in the right direction is more than necessary .

EXERCISES:

WAYS TO CORRECT CHILDREN'S MISTAKES:

1. Mistake is not a bad word. It is not a crime to do something wrong. The important thing to take note of is

the experience we gather from the mistake. Parents should show their children how to learn from one's mistakes.

2. Only by imparting love can we make our children be better people. Explaining things by caressing fondly has the power of modifying the unpleasant things done by them.

3. The way we reprimand children when they commit mistakes and then give them a chance to redeem the same, we must shower them with appreciation and words of praise when they do good deeds .

4. Teach children the importance of planning in different phases of life. If they do not inculcate this habit, then, at different stages of life, they make the same mistake over and over again, unknowingly .

5. Think carefully about each action of yours before taking a decision. Accept the new opportunities that come your way. They should be conducive to your journey.

6. The experience derived from the mistakes you made will make you understand yourself better. Your mistakes will make you realise your own worth.

7. A mistake will highlight your fears, weaknesses and shortcomings. It will also make you understand if anything needs to be fixed within you.

8. Just the way you claim your success, admit your mistakes. It will reveal your maturity. Admitting one's mistakes needs bravery. It will also prevent you from repeating the same mistake again.

9. Never compare your children with other children, especially about academics or talents. This generally induces emotions like anger and mental stress. It makes them feel less special than their peers. They start looking down on themselves out of inferiority complex.

10. If you promise something to your children , then make sure that you fulfil your promise earnestly. This will

deepen their confidence and trust in you.

About Author

Author other books:

Language : Tamil

Book Name: Petrokal Marantatum - Pillaikal Maruppatum

Prize : Rs.200

Available : Amazon, Flipkart & Notion press

Get in touch and send him your reviews:

WhatsApp: + 91 8870795112

Email: alanjoseph.joseph96@gmail.com

YouTube: https://www.youtube.com/channel/UCy5tfWDRAWje15JVrZnjijw

LinkedIn : https://www.linkedin.com/in/alan-joseph-6091607a

Facebook: https://www.facebook.com/profile.php?id=100008969223711

Services offered for,

- Offering an individual counselling for psychological and emotional problems.
- Training and workshops are providing in different topics based on their needs for families, students, youth, parents and staffs.